Birthday gift from Evelyn Kent

ELLIS ISLAND

11/28/95

Re-gifted to George from Char 5/2/06

ELLIS ISLAND

GEORGES PEREC WITH ROBERT BOBER

TRANSLATED FROM THE FRENCH BY HARRY MATHEWS
"Remembrances" translated from the French by Jessica Blatt

THE NEW PRESS
NEW YORK

Originally published in French as
Récits d'Ellis Island: histoires d'errance et d'espoir by P.O.L
éditeur, Paris, France, copyright © 1994 P.O.L éditeur
English translations by Harry Mathews and Jessica Blatt
© 1995 by The New Press

Library of Congress Catalog Card Number 95-70944
ISBN 1-56584-318-5

Originally published in French by P.O.L, Paris
Published in the United States by The New Press, New York
Distributed by W. W. Norton & Company, Inc., New York

Established in 1990 as a major alternative to the large,
commercial publishing houses, The New Press is the first
full-scale nonprofit American book publisher outside
of the university presses. The Press is operated editorially
in the public interest, rather than for private gain;
it is committed to publishing in innovative ways works
of educational, cultural, and community value that,
despite their intellectual merits, might not normally
be commercially viable. The New Press's editorial offices
are located at the City University of New York.

Book design by Jean Lagarrigue
Composition by Jean Poderos

Production management by Kim Waymer
Printed in the United States of America

95 96 97 98   9 8 7 6 5 4 3 2 1

CONTENTS

A Paris, quand nous disions que nous
allions faire un film sur Ellis
Island, presque tout le monde nous
demandait de quoi il s'agissait.
A New York, presque tout le monde
nous demandait pourquoi. Non
pas pourquoi un film à propos d'Ellis
Island, mais pourquoi nous. En
quoi cela nous concernait-il, nous,
Robert Bober et Georges Perec ?

Il serait sans doute un peu artificiel
de dire que nous avons réalisé ce film
à seule fin de comprendre pourquoi
nous avions le désir ou le besoin de
le faire. Il faudra bien, pourtant,
que les images qui vont suivre
répondent à ces deux questions, et
décrivent, non seulement ce lieu
unique, mais le chemin qui nous
y a conduits.

Robert Bober and Georges Perec,
New York Harbor, 1979

To the memory of Madame Kamer.

The country we call our own is this poor shore
where we find ourselves stranded.
—Jean-Paul de Dadelsen, *Jonas*

Previous page:

Whenever we told people in Paris that we were planning
a film on Ellis Island, the question nearly everyone
asked was: what is it about? In New York, the usual
question was why—not why a film on Ellis Island,
but why us? What did the subject have to do with the
two of us, with either Robert Bober or Georges Perec?

It would be forcing the truth to say that our aim in
making this film was to find out why we wanted
and needed to make it. All the same, the images and
text that follow will be obliged to deal not only
with Ellis Island and what it was but with our own
itinerary in getting there.

1. THE ISLE OF TEARS

THE ISLE OF TEARS

Duuring the first half of the nineteenth century, a tremendous hope
galvanized Europe. For peoples that were crushed, oppressed,
downtrodden, enslaved, or butchered, for classes that were exploited,
starved, afflicted by epidemics, or decimated by years of scarcity
and famine, a promised land came into existence: America, a virgin land
open to all, a land of freedom and generosity where the castoffs of the
Old World could become the pioneers of the New and build a society free
of injustice and prejudice. For Irish peasants whose harvests had been
ruined, for the persecuted German liberals of 1848, for the battered Polish
nationalists of 1830, for Armenians, Greeks, and Turks, for all the Jews
of Russia and the Austro-Hungarian Empire, for southern Italians dying
from cholera and poverty by the hundreds of thousands, America
became the symbol of a new life, of long-awaited luck; and it was by
the tens of millions, by entire families and villages that, from Hamburg or
Bremen, from Le Havre, from Naples or Liverpool, immigrants embarked
on a voyage of no return.

For several decades the terminal point of this exodus without
precedent in human history, the end of a crossing almost invariably

THE ISLE OF TEARS

accomplished in appalling conditions, was a tiny spot of land
called Ellis Island, where the services of the Federal Bureau
of Immigration had established their reception center.
And so it came about that on this narrow sandbank in the mouth
of the Hudson, a few cable lengths away from the brand-new
Statue of Liberty, there gathered together for a time all those who
were destined to create the American nation.

More or less free until about 1875, the admission of
foreigners onto American soil was gradually subjected
to restrictive measures, initially defined and applied locally
(by port or municipal authorities) and later centralized
in a bureau of immigration responsible to the federal
government. The opening of the Ellis Island reception center
in 1892 marked the end of virtually unregulated immigration
and the advent of official, institutionalized and,
so to speak, industrialized immigration. Between 1892
and 1924, nearly sixteen million people passed through
Ellis Island, at a rate of five to ten thousand a day.
The majority spent a few hours there; no more than two to three
per cent were turned away.

Essentially, Ellis Island was a sort of factory for
manufacturing Americans,* a factory for transforming emigrants
into immigrants; an American-style factory, as quick and
efficient as a sausage factory in Chicago. You put an Irishman,
a Ukranian Jew, or an Italian from Apulia into one end of the

* Seventy per cent of
European immigrants
entered through New York.

12

production line and at the other end—after vaccination, disinfection, and examination of his eyes and pockets— an American emerged. But at the same time, as the years passed, admission became more and more strictly controlled. Gradually the Golden Door swung shut on the legendary America where turkeys fell onto your plate fully cooked, where the streets were paved with gold, where the land belonged to everyone. Immigration slowed down, in fact, after 1914, initially because of the war, later because of a series of discriminatory measures both qualitative (the Literacy Act) and quantitative (the quota system) that virtually denied entrance to the "wretched refuse" and "huddled masses" whom, according to Emma Lazarus, the Statue of Liberty was meant to welcome. In 1924 the responsibility for immigration procedures was transferred to the American consulates in Europe; Ellis Island was reduced to the status of detention center for those immigrants whose papers were not in order.

During and immediately after World War II, Ellis Island fulfilled its implicit destiny by becoming a prison for individuals suspected of anti-American activities (Italian fascists, pro-Nazi Germans, communists, and supposed communists). It was definitively closed in 1954. Today it has become a historic landmark, like Mount Rushmore, Old Faithful, and Bartholdi's statue, managed by Rangers in Boy Scout hats who conduct tours through it four times a day, twelve months a year.

Not all immigrants were obliged to pass through Ellis Island. Those with enough money to travel first or second class were quickly examined on board ship by a doctor and an immigration officer and could land without further ado. The federal government assumed that these immigrants had the wherewithal to look after themselves and were not likely to become wards of the state. The immigrants who went to Ellis Island were those who traveled third class, that is, in steerage, which in fact meant below the water line in the hold, in vast dormitories not only without windows but practically without ventilation or lighting,

where two thousand passengers were crammed together on tiers of straw mattresses. The trip cost ten dollars in the 1880s and thirty-five dollars after World War I. It lasted about three weeks. The food consisted of potatoes and salt herring.

A whole series of official procedures took place during the crossing. These were performed by the shipping companies, who were more or less responsible for the passengers they took aboard—they had to pay for their passengers' living expenses on Ellis Island, and they were obliged to repatriate any emigrants who were turned away. The procedures included a medical examination (usually bungled), disinfections, vaccinations, and the establishment of a personal record for each emigrant that listed his name, country of origin, destination, means, judicial record, sponsor in the United States, and so forth.

On Ellis Island itself the examination procedures lasted at best from three to five hours. The arrivals first underwent a medical examination. Any doubtful case was detained and subjected to a much more thorough medical inspection; a number of contagious diseases, particularly trachoma, favus, and tuberculosis, meant automatic expulsion. Emigrants who emerged from this examination unscathed were then asked, after a waiting period of variable length, to appear at the legal desks. Behind each of these sat an inspector and an interpreter. (For many years Fiorello La Guardia, before becoming mayor of New York, was an interpreter in Yiddish and Italian on Ellis Island.) The inspector had about two minutes in which to decide whether or not the emigrant had a right to enter the United States. He made his decision after asking a series of twenty-nine questions:

What is your name?
Where are you from?
Why have you come to the United States?
How old are you?

How much money do you have?
Where did you get this money?
Show it to me.
Who paid for your crossing?
Did you sign a contract in Europe for a job here?
Do you have any friends here?
Do you have any family here?
Is there anyone who can vouch for you?
What kind of work do you do?
Are you an anarchist?
   —and so forth.

If the new arrival answered in a manner that was deemed satisfactory, the inspector would stamp his papers and let him leave, after wishing him "Welcome to America." If there was any kind of problem, he wrote an "S.I." on the arrival's record. This stood for Special Inquiry, and after another waiting period the arrival would be summoned before a committee made up of three inspectors, who subjected the would-be immigrant to a far more detailed interrogation.

In 1917, overriding President Wilson's veto, Congress passed the Literacy Act, which required immigrants to be able to read and write in their native language and also obliged them to take various intelligence tests. The system was already unfavorable to the new emigrants from eastern Europe, Russia, and Italy. (Those who arrived during the first three-quarters of the nineteenth century had come from the Scandinavian

817. Embarking Emigrants at Docks, Genoa, Italy.

and Italy. (Those who arrived during the first three-quarters of the nineteenth century had come from the Scandinavian countries, Germany, Holland, England, and Ireland). These new measures made the admission procedure even longer and, from one year to the next, much more difficult.

The majority of the inspectors did their work conscientiously and, with the help of their interpreters, did their best to obtain exact information from the new arrivals. A great many of them were of Irish origin and had little familiarity with the spelling and pronunciation of the names of central Europe, Russia, Greece, or Turkey. Furthermore, many emigrants hoped to acquire names that sounded American. Hence the innumerable incidents of name changes that occurred on Ellis Island. A man from Berlin became Berliner; another whose first name was Vladimir received Walter as his given name; a man whose first name was Adam became Mr. Adams; a Skyzertski was transformed into Sanders, a Goldenburg into Goldberg, and a Gold became Goldstein.

Embarking emigrants at docks, Genoa, Italy.

18

Registering Jewish passengers in the emigrants waiting room in Hamburg-Veddel, 1909.

One old Russian Jew was advised to pick a truly American name, one that the immigration authorities would have no difficulty in transcribing. He asked the advice of an employee in the baggage room who suggested Rockefeller. The old Jew kept repeating "Rockefeller, Rockefeller" to be sure he'd remember. But several hours later, when the immigration officer asked him his name, he had forgotten it and answered in Yiddish, "Schon vergessen"— "I've already forgotten." And so he was registered with the truly American name of John Ferguson.

THE ISLE OF TEARS

The story is perhaps too good to be true, but ultimately it hardly matters whether it's true or false. To emigrants yearning for America, a new name might seem a blessing. For their grandchildren today, things are different. It is remarkable that in 1976, the Bicentennial year, several dozen Smiths whose families had come from Poland asked to be renamed Kowalski (both names mean blacksmith).

No more than two per cent of all emigrants were turned away from Ellis Island. That still amounts to two hundred and fifty thousand people. And between 1892 and 1924, there were three thousand suicides on Ellis Island.

2. THE WAY TO ELLIS ISLAND

*S*h! We're going to America! Where's America? I don't know. I only know that it's awfully far away. You have to travel and travel a very long time to get there. And when you get there, there's a "Kestelgartel*" waiting for you. They shut you up in the "Kestelgartel," they take off all your clothes and examine your eyes. If your eyes are healthy, it's all right. If they aren't, they make you go back to where you came from. As far as I know, my eyes are healthy.... On the other hand, as my brother Eliahu says, things aren't so easy for my mother. Who's responsible? She cries day and night. Ever since father died, she hasn't stopped crying.

SHOLOM ALEICHEM,
The Adventures of Mottell,
the Cantor's Son

* Castle Garden

THE WAY TO ELLIS ISLAND

five million emigrants arriving from Italy

four million emigrants arriving from Ireland

one million emigrants arriving from Sweden

six million emigrants arriving from Germany

three million emigrants arriving from Austria and Hungary

three million five hundred thousand emigrants arriving
from Russia and the Ukraine

five million emigrants arriving from Great Britain

eight hundred thousand emigrants arriving from Norway

six hundred thousand emigrants arriving from Greece

four hundred thousand emigrants arriving from Turkey

*Left: Castle Garden, where
the first emigrants arrived.*

four hundred thousand emigrants arriving from the Netherlands

*Next page, double spread:
Emigrants' departure hall
at Hamburg-Veddel.
On the wall is inscribed:
"The world is my field."*

six hundred thousand emigrants arriving from France

three hundred thousand emigrants arriving from Denmark

The Blücher, an emigrant ship,
leaves Hamburg (around 1909)

Un bateau d'émigrants,
Blücher, quitte Hambourg
(vers 1909)

THE WAY TO ELLIS ISLAND

year after year, the steamships of
the Cunard Line, the Red Star Line,
the Anchor Line, the Italian Line, the Hamburg-
Amerika Line, and the Holland-America Line
crisscrossed the North Atlantic

they set out from Rotterdam, from Bremen
and Göteborg, from Palermo, Istanbul, and Naples,
from Antwerp, Liverpool, Lübeck, and Salonika,
from Bristol, Riga, Cork, from Dunkirk, Stettin, and
Hamburg, from Marseille, Genoa, Danzig, Cherbourg, and the
Piraeus, from Trieste and London, from Fiume
and Le Havre, from Odessa, from Tallinn, from Southampton

they were called the Darmstadt, the Fürst Bismarck,
the Staatendam, the Kaiser Wilhelm, the Königin Luise,
the Westernland, the Pennland,
the Bohemia, the Polynesia, the Prinzess Irene, the Princeton,
the Umbria, the Lusitania, the Adriatic,
the Coronia, the Mauretania, the San Giovanni,
the Giuseppe Verdi, the Patricia, the Duca degli Abruzzi,
the New Amsterdam, the Martha Washington,
the Thuringia, the Titanic,
the Lidia, the Susquehanna, the Albert Balin,
the Hansington, the Columbus, the Reliance, the Blücher

A bord du Pennland (Red Star Line) (1893)   *Aboard the Pennland (Red Star Line) (1893)*

THE WAY TO ELLIS ISLAND

but at the conclusion of their exhausting
journey, most of those who saw Manhattan
emerging from the mist knew that their ordeal
was not quite over

they still had to pass through Ellis Island,
the island that
in every European tongue
had been renamed the isle of tears

tränen insel

wispa łez

île des larmes

isola delle lagrime

το νησί των δαχρύων

остров слёз

טרערן-אינדזל

Aboard the Westernland (1890?)

A bord du Westernland (1890?)

30

THE WAY TO ELLIS ISLAND

designed in the style of the French Renaissance
by the architects Boring and Tilton,
left to rack and ruin since 1954,
the buildings on Ellis Island were declared
part of the Statue of Liberty National Monument
in 1976, the year of the Bicentenary,
and reopened to the public.

But emigration to the United States
began long before Ellis Island
and did not end when it closed down.

Mexicans, Cubans, Koreans,
Vietnamese, and Cambodians have taken up
where the others left off

THE WAY TO ELLIS ISLAND

it was on Wednesday, May 31, 1978,
that Robert Bober and I first visited Ellis Island.
On the same tour were a couple in their
fifties (the wife's mother, who had recently died,
had passed through Ellis Island)
and a very young woman who carried
in her arms a baby only a few days old

I doubt that anyone visits Ellis Island by chance these days.
People who passed through it have little desire to return—
their children or grandchildren do it for them, looking
for traces of the past. What had been for the others a place
of trials and uncertainties has become for them a place
of recollection, a pivot of the connections that identify
them with their history.

THE WAY TO ELLIS ISLAND

how can things be described?

or talked about?

or looked at?

beyond dry official statistics,
beyond the reassuring drone of stories
that have been told a thousand times
by guides in their Boy Scout hats,
beyond the official display of everyday objects
that have become museum pieces, the stuff of history,
precious vestiges, venerable images,

beyond the artificial calm of these photographs,
fixed forever in their misleading
black-and-white obviousness

how can you identify this place?

how do you reconstruct it?

how do you decipher these relics?

how do you move beyond,
           move behind
           not rest content with what we're given to see
           not merely see what we knew we would in advance?

How can you grasp what isn't shown, what wasn't photographed
or catalogued or restored or staged?

How do you get back what was plain, trivial, routine,
what was ordinary and kept happening day after day?

The Ellis Island infirmary in 1979.

Nous avons arpenté des dizaines
et des dizaines de couloirs,
visité des dizaines et des
dizaines de salles, des pièces
de toutes dimensions, des halls,
des bureaux, des chambres,
des buanderies, des toilettes,
des cagibis, des débarras,
et chaque fois en nous demandant
en essayant de vous représenter,
ce qui s'y passait, à quoi ça
ressemblait, qui venait là, et
pourquoi, qui parcourait ces
couloirs, qui montait ces
escaliers, qui attendait sur
ces bancs,
comment s'écoulaient ces heures
et ces jours,
comment faisaient tous ces
gens pour se nourrir, se laver,
se coucher, s'habiller ?

Cela ne veut rien dire, de vouloir
faire parler ces images, de les
forcer à dire ce qu'elles ne
sauraient dire.

Au début, on ne peut qu'essayer
de nommer les choses, une
à une, platement,
les énumérer, les dénombrer,
de la manière la plus
banale possible
de la manière la plus précise
possible,
en essayant de ne rien
oublier.

THE WAY TO ELLIS ISLAND

We walked down dozens
and dozens of corridors,
we visited dozens and
dozens of rooms, rooms
of every size, waiting rooms,
offices, dormitories,
laundries, latrines,
storerooms, larders,
each time trying to imagine
what had happened there, what it
had looked like, who had been there
and why—who had gone along
these corridors, or up these stairs,
or had waited on
these benches,
how were the hours spent,
and the days?
how did all these
people manage to eat, wash,
sleep, and dress?

it's pointless wanting to
make pictures speak,
forcing them to say
what they can't.

for a start, you can only try
to name things, one
at a time, unemphatically,
listing them, counting them
in the plainest
possible way,
in the most precise
possible way,
doing your best
to leave nothing out.

Georges Perec at Ellis Island in 1979.

THE WAY TO ELLIS ISLAND

for example:

a large white porcelain double sink,
with a hand-cranked spin dryer resting in it

four chairs

two ironing boards set on thick cast-iron legs,
one with a rectangular, the other with an oval base;
on one ironing board is an electric iron;
on the other stand the remains of a sleeve-board
covered in striped material like mattress ticking;

three sewing machines, two of which
—a Singer and a White Rotary—
are still intact

and two thirds of the way up the wall
two long boards screwed into the tiles,
still retaining a suggestion of clothes-lines

46

THE WAY TO ELLIS ISLAND

this is what you see today,
and the one thing we know
is that this is not
the way it was
at the turn of the
century

but this is what is left for us to see,
and we have nothing else
to exhibit

THE WAY TO ELLIS ISLAND

nothing looks as much like a forsaken place
as another forsaken place

this could be a storeroom anywhere
any abandoned factory
any vacated depot
consumed by dampness and rust,

warehouses that have collapsed,
mills where for ages no wheels have turned,
derelict granaries, silos overrun
with weeds

49

THE WAY TO ELLIS ISLAND

once again the guide is giving his account
of the emigrants' arrival, how they climbed the stairs,
the medical checkups, the eye tests, the letters chalked
on the shoulders of the possibly sick, the endless waiting,
the rapid-fire list of twenty-nine questions

he walks back and forth as he speaks,
and the visitors watch him

they've known these stories forever

they know that when Irving Berlin arrived at Ellis Island
he was called Israel Beilin,
that Samuel Goldwyn came through Ellis Island
as well as Ben Shahn,
and that Fiorello LaGuardia was an interpreter here

they've heard the story of Schon Vergessen
and the one about the three brothers
who in turn received the names
Appletree, Applebaum, and Appleberg

they haven't come to learn anything
but to recover something,
to participate in something particularly theirs,

some indelible trace of their story

something that is part of their common memory
and that in their innermost self has forged
their consciousness of being American

THE WAY TO ELLIS ISLAND

as for the rest, we can only try to imagine it,
deducing it from what has survived and been preserved,
from what has been saved from destruction and
oblivion

and the question can at last be asked: what did this place
mean to all those who passed through it

what quantities of hope, expectation, daring,
enthusiasm, and energy were accumulated here

rather than simply saying: in thirty years
sixteen million emigrants passed through Ellis Island

attempting to give palpable form
to what those sixteen million individual stories were,
the sixteen million stories, identical and distinct,
of the men, women, and children driven
from their native land by famine or poverty,
or by political, racial, or religious oppression,
leaving everything behind—village, family, friends—
taking months and years to set aside
the money needed for the trip,
finding themselves here, in a hall so vast that they never
would have dared imagine that there could anywhere
exist so big a place,
lined up by fours,
waiting their turn

THE WAY TO ELLIS ISLAND

the point is not to have pity, but understanding

four emigrants out of five
spent no more than a few hours on Ellis Island

it was really nothing more than an innocuous formality,
the time needed to change an emigrant into an immigrant,
someone who had left into someone who had arrived,

but to every one of those
who marched past the doctors and immigration officers,
what was at stake was vital:

they had given up their past and their history,
they had given up everything for the sake of coming here
to try and live a life they were forbidden to live
in their native land:
and now they were face to face with an inexorable finality

THE WAY TO ELLIS ISLAND

what we see today is a chaotic assemblage of things,
the remnants of alterations, demolitions,
and restorations

objects piled helter-skelter, stacks of gratings,
sections of scaffolding, junked spotlights

tables, desks, rusted lockers, and
filing cabinets, bedsteads, bits of wood,
benches, rolls of tarpaper,
everything and anything:
a large saucepan, a sieve,
a mobile fire pump, a coffee pot, an adding machine,
an electric fan, glass jars, cafeteria trays,
lead piping, a wheelbarrow, the remains of a hand truck,
unfilled forms, a hymnal,
paper cups, some kind of board game.

THE WAY TO ELLIS ISLAND

Ellis Island was ravaged
not only by time,
dampness, and salt air
but by plunder:
for almost twenty years, the little island, no longer in use
and left virtually unguarded, was systematically ransacked
by dealers in scrap metal, who came looking for materials
that were growing more valuable with every passing year:
brass from faucets and doorknobs,
zinc from the roofing,
lead from the plumbing,
wrought iron from banisters,
bronze from lamp stands and overhead lights,
they took everything they could pile onto their boats,
leaving to rot where they lay the masses of furniture,
the piles of mattresses and rusty bedsprings,
the mounds of burst pillows

THE WAY TO ELLIS ISLAND

why are we telling these stories?

what did we come here to find?

what did we come here to ask?

removed from us in space and in time, this place
belongs to a memory potentially
our own,
to a probable autobiography.
our parents or grandparents might have been here
it was mainly chance that decided whether they would stay
or would not stay in Poland, whether they would stop
on the way, in Germany
or Austria or England or France.

THE WAY TO ELLIS ISLAND

to each of us, this shared fate has appeared
in a different light:

what I, Georges Perec, have come here to examine
is dispersion, wandering, diaspora.
To me Ellis Island is the ultimate place of exile, that is,
the place where place is absent, the non-place,
the nowhere.
it is in light of this that these pictures concern
and fascinate and involve me,
as if the search for my own identity
depended on my incorporating this dumping-ground
where frazzled bureaucrats baptized
Americans in droves.
what I find present here
are in no way landmarks or roots or
relics
but their opposite: something shapeless, on the outer edge of
what is sayable,
something that might be called closure, or cleavage,
or severance,
and that in my mind is linked
in a most intimate and confused way
with the very fact of being a Jew

THE WAY TO ELLIS ISLAND

I don't know exactly what it is
to be a Jew,
or what effect being a Jew has on me

there's something obvious about it, I suppose,
but it's a worthless obviousness
that doesn't connect me with anything.
it isn't a sign of belonging,
it doesn't have to do with belief, or religion, or a code
of behavior, a way of life, or a language;
it seems more like a silence, a deficiency, a question,
a questioning, a dubiousness, an uneasiness:

an uneasy certainty,
and looming behind that, another certainty,
abstract, oppressive, and intolerable:
that of having been labeled a Jew,
Jew therefore victim,
and so beholden for being alive to exile and luck

THE WAY TO ELLIS ISLAND

like near and distant cousins of mine,
I might have been born
in Haifa, Baltimore, or Vancouver
I might have been Argentinean, Australian, English or
Swedish,
but in the almost unlimited range of
possibilities,
one thing was specifically denied me:
I could not be born in the country of my ancestors,
in Lubartow or Warsaw,
or grow up there, in the continuity of tradition,
language, and community.

In some way I'm estranged
from myself;
in some way I'm "different," not different from others
but from "my own people":
I don't speak the language my parents spoke,
I share none of the memories they may have had,
something that was theirs and made them what they were
—their story, their culture, their hope—
was not handed down to me.

THE WAY TO ELLIS ISLAND

I don't have the feeling that I've forgotten
but that I was never allowed to learn;
this is how my approach differs
from Robert Bober's:

to him, being Jewish means continuing to reaffirm one's place
in a tradition, a language, a culture, and
a community that neither centuries of diaspora
nor the systematic genocide of the "final solution"
succeeded in definitively crushing;

to him, being Jewish means inheriting and then passing on
an entire body of customs,
ways of eating, dancing, and singing, of words,
tastes, and habits,

and above all it's the sense of sharing
these acts and rites with others, regardless of boundaries and
nationalities, and these shared things become roots,
it's obvious how essential and fragile they are,
threatened as always by time and by man.

fragments of memory and forgetfulness, gestures that are
rediscovered without ever having been learned, words that come
back, memories of lullabies,

photographs lovingly kept:
signs of belonging where he sinks
his roots in history, that enable him to fashion
his identity; that is, what makes him
both himself and identical with others.

Wolf Leib Frankel,
Robert Bober's great-grandfather,
shipped back from
Ellis Island for trachoma

THE WAY TO ELLIS ISLAND

It was to test the permanence of his traditions,
their durability, their tenacity, their resilience,
that Robert Bober came to Ellis Island,

as well as to retrieve, from traces left by the people
who passed through here and from the testimony we planned
to gather from them, the image of his mother's grandfather, who
in 1900 left his village in Poland
to go to America but caught trachoma on the crossing
and was shipped back.

THE WAY TO ELLIS ISLAND

Perhaps the Jews, a people without a country,
condemned almost from their origins to exodus and survival
among cultures different from their own,
may have been more aware than others
of what was at stake for them;

but Ellis Island was never a place restricted to Jews

it belongs to all those whom intolerance and poverty
have driven and still drive from the land where they
grew up

at a time when boat people still keep going from one island to the
next in search of ever more unlikely havens,
it might seem ludicrous or pointless
or sentimentally self-indulgent to want to recall these tales
from an already distant past

but in doing so, we were sure of having resoundingly evoked the
two words that lie at the very heart of this long venture: two
intangible, precarious, weak, fugitive words that keep endlessly
refracting each other's wavering light and whose names are
wandering and hope.

THE WAY TO ELLIS ISLAND

from *Amerika* by Franz Kafka

*As Karl Rossmann, a poor boy of sixteen…stood on the liner
slowly entering the harbor of New York, a sudden burst
of sunshine seemed to illumine the Statue of Liberty, so that
he saw it in a new light, although he had sighted it long
before. The arm with the sword rose up as if newly stretched
aloft, and round the figure blew the free winds of heaven.*

THE WAY TO ELLIS ISLAND

being an emigrant may have meant
exactly that: seeing a sword
where the sculptor had, in all good faith, designed
a torch—
and not being altogether mistaken

on the base of the Statue of Liberty are engraved
the famous lines of Emma Lazarus

Give me your tired, your poor,
Your huddled masses yearning to breathe free,
The wretched refuse of your teeming shore,
Send these, the homeless, tempest-tossed, to me,
I lift my lamp beside the Golden Door!

but at that very moment a whole series of laws was being enacted
to control and later compress
the influx of emigrants

from one year to the next the conditions of entry became more
and more stringent, and the doors gradually swung shut on
that legendary America, the El Dorado of modern times, where
—as little children in Europe were told—the streets were
paved with gold, and the land was so vast and bountiful that
there was room in it for everyone

Next page: Immigrants
leaving Ellis Island
to enter the United States

THE WAY TO ELLIS ISLAND

four million immigrants came from Ireland

four hundred thousand immigrants came from Turkey
and Armenia

five million immigrants came from Sicily and Italy

six million immigrants came from Germany

four hundred thousand immigrants came from Holland

three million immigrants came from Austria and Hungary

six hundred thousand immigrants came from Greece

six hundred thousand immigrants came from Bohemia
and Moravia

three million five hundred thousand immigrants came from
Russia and the Ukraine

one million immigrants came from Sweden

three hundred thousand immigrants came from Romania
and Bulgaria

for immigrants disembarking for the first time at Battery Park, it didn't take long to realize that what they had been told about America the Beautiful was not entirely accurate: the land might belong to everyone, but those who had arrived first had already helped themselves liberally; the only thing left for them to do was bundle themselves ten to a room into the windowless slums of the Lower East Side and start working fifteen hours a day. Turkeys didn't tumble onto their plates fully cooked, and the streets of New York were not paved with gold—in fact, most of them weren't paved at all. And they then understood that it was precisely in order to pave them that they had been brought over: to pave streets, to dig tunnels and canals, to build roads, bridges, giant dams and railroads, to clear forests, to work mines and quarries, to manufacture automobiles and cigars, carbines and three-piece suits, shoes, chewing gum, corned beef, and soap, and to raise skyscrapers even higher than those they had gazed on at their arrival.

3. ALBUM

Landing (1907)

Arriving at Ellis Island. The immigrants hold their registration cards in
their teeth. Behind them is the ferry that shuttled
back and forth between Ellis Island and the tip of Manhattan.
(See pages 108-109 for the same ferry in 1979.)

Italian family aboard the Immigration Services ferry.

Family of Italian immigrants (1905).

*Russian Jew at Ellis Island (1905). Russian Jews began emigrating
around 1840. Pogroms and the Russo-Japanese War of 1905 led to the
second wave of emigration.*
*Today it is estimated that there are two million Jews
of Russian origin living in the United States.*

Young Russian-Jewish woman at Ellis Island (1905).

Jewish grandmother at Ellis Island (1926).

A little Italian girl receives her first penny (1926).

Russian mother with her children in the registration hall (1905).

Behind this Italian mother and her child can be seen the hall where 1,700 immigrants crowded into a space intended for 600.

84

One of the many inspections to which new arrivals were subjected.

Slavic immigrant woman at Ellis Island (1905).

Dr. O'Connor examining Irish immigrants (around 1930).

A stranger receives us
Harshly and asks: "And your health?"
He examines us. His look
Assesses us like dogs.

He studies in depth
Eyes and mouth. No doubt
That if he'd probed our hearts
He would have seen the wound.

AVROM REISEN,
The First Immigrants

*The main registration hall. It was derisively referred to as "the cattle pen"
because of the railings that divided it into corridors. Judged to be inhuman,
the railings were removed in 1911 and replaced with benches.
(See photograph on the following page.)*

Children undergoing a medical examination at the time of a typhus scare (1911).

The last steps to America (1905).

With train tickets pinned to their lapels,
a German family prepares to leave Ellis Island.

The last formality behind them, immigrants here converted their money into dollars. Not knowing what American money looked like, they often let themselves be swindled by the cashiers, who would sometimes give them other foreign currencies in exchange.

Production still (1979).

4. ON LOCATION

ON LOCATION

We made a preliminary trip to New York during the first half of June 1978.

All we then knew of Ellis Island was a few old photographs. Our plans were first to get to know a place that was still an abstraction, then prepare the shooting of the film, scheduled at the time for the fall.

We brought several dozen addresses with us from Paris. Our notebooks were soon stuffed with more names, addresses, and telephone numbers: people to see, institutions to contact, information to ask for, formalities to attend to.

Between archival research, meeting people who'd known Ellis Island and were willing to talk about it (something that, for one reason or another, could not be taken for granted), and our visits to the island, our days were spent making innumerable phone calls, walking down avenues to the point of exhaustion, waiting, trying to find addresses, and studying itineraries; doing all this in a state of confusion and uncertainty that became inextricably associated with our idea of New York and of which the lists that follow, drawn up immediately after our return to France, may convey an adequate notion:

ON LOCATION

PEOPLE WE SAW

Maxine Groffsky, Kate Manheim, Richard Foreman, Babette
Mangolte, Samuel Heilman, Dinah Abramowicz, Simon and Olive
Liberman, Bill and Pat Lievow, Nancy Nicholas, David Moffitt,
Françoise Kourilsky, John Blum, Baruch Chasimow, Emily Weiss
and her friends, Roselyn Schwartz, Morris Merow and his wife,
Dr. Weinbaum, Ellen Bishop, Nathan Solomon and his wife,
Nelsie Gidney's assistant, the secretary at Elia Kazan's New York
office, John Ware, Louie Balducci, Nelsie Gidney, Tom Bishop,
Jack and Frances Doniger, Tom Bernardin.

PEOPLE WE DIDN'T SEE BUT THAT WE SHOULD,
COULD, OR WOULD HAVE LIKED TO SEE

Carolyn Tumarkin, John Ashbery, Ruth and Archie Perlmutter,
Kenneth Libo, Mr. Staiwkowski, Sonia and David Landes,
Simone Arnold, Denise Wise, Jacques and Estelle Bienenfeld,
Sandy Lerman, Norma Silverman, Jerome Rothenberg, Richard
Howard, Edmund White, Anne Marie Cunningham, Amy and
Peter Bernstein, Peter Israël, Maurice Sendak, Arthur Gold,
Robert Fizdale, Chantal and John Willett, Elliott Stein, Frances
Scalon, Paul Buhle, Alice Kessler-Harris, Florence Stafford,
the woman who edits *Forward!*, Isidore Gorenstein, Fanny
Koltman, Molly Rothberg, Epp Kotkas, Sassoon Soffer, Esther
Brumberg, Joan Morrison, Walter Betkowski, Jonas Mekas,
Mr. Spanel, Joe Brainard, Father Tomasi, etc.

ON LOCATION

PLACES

John F. Kennedy Airport, Air Terminal, Bus Terminal
Abbey Victoria Hotel
Algonquin Hotel, Chelsea Hotel, Gramercy Park Hotel
Grand Central Station
General Post Office
a dozen apartments and lofts
the New York offices of French television
the offices of Channel Thirteen
Elia Kazan's New York office
The YIVO Institute for Jewish Research
Tamiment Library of New York University
Ellis Island

The Statue of Liberty

the World Trade Center, the Empire State Building,
Rockefeller Center,
Lincoln Center, the Time-Life building, the Village, Soho,
Central Park,
Staten Island, 42nd Street, Second Avenue, Park Avenue,
Fifth Avenue, Seventh Avenue, Sixth Avenue, Broadway,
the Lower East Side, Roselyn Schwartz's childhood house,

the Whitney Museum (the Steinberg exhibition)
the Guggenheim Museum, the Jewish Museum,

ON LOCATION

the Frick Collection, the Museum of the City of New York,
the American Museum of Immigration,
the New York Public Library

VARIOUS EVENTS

Puerto Rican parade down Fifth Avenue
Italian street fair in the parish of St. Anthony of Padua
(McDougal Street)
Games and concerts in Central Park
Games and concerts in Washington Square
Exhibition of Babette Mangolte's photographs
(P.S. 1 in Queens)
Stage show at Radio City Music Hall
Pianists (Empire Diner, Gramercy Park Hotel)
Destination America (BBC film on immigration)
Innumerable bits of movies on the television set in our
hotel bedroom

The film crew. From left to right: Georges Perec,
Jean-Claude Brisson, Robert Bober, Claude Pezet, and Jacques Pamart.

RESTAURANTS, COFFEE SHOPS, BARS, ETC.

Wolf's Sixth Avenue Delicatessen, Austrian restaurant,
One Fifth, Italian restaurant on Second Avenue, Italian
restaurant in Soho, other restaurants in Soho, Café Figaro,
Empire Diner, Jewish restaurant on Second Avenue,
Promenade Bar in Rockefeller Center, terrace of Central
Park Café, terrace at Lincoln Center, various bars,
various delis, various coffee shops (Abbey Victoria Hotel,
Hotel Americana, Time-Life building, etc.)

ON LOCATION

FOOD

spaghetti and meat balls, chicken "cordon bleu," various
kinds of lasagne, blintzes, tunafish salad, chef's salad,
prosciutto with melon, tortellini, fettucine, chocolate cake,
cheesecake, spare ribs, taramasalata, pastrami, tongue,
salami, cantaloupe, gefilte fish, hamburgers, franks, etc.

SHOPS

museum gift shops, postcard shops, camera shops, tobacco
shops, bookstores, record stores, five-and-dime stores, etc.

PURCHASES (AMONG OTHERS)

crunchy candies, frisbees, stamps, Bufferin, writing pads,
postcards, toothpaste, etc.

5. REMEMBRANCES

Two old Jewish men
on a ferry with Manhattan
in the background.

REMEMBRANCES

For two out of three immigrants, New York was no more than a way station. Those who did try to settle there usually found themselves faced with living and working conditions even harder than those they had known in their home countries. Some were to succeed in making their fortunes, adding their stories to the golden myth of the American dream. The majority spent the rest of their lives working and managed to improve their lot.

We met several of those who lived this adventure. The youngest is now sixty-one years of age; the oldest is ninety-six. We made no attempt at a representative sampling. Rather, we limited ourselves to two communities, Italian and Jewish, because these were the groups that were most involved with Ellis Island and because we felt closest to them personally.

The filming took place during the entire month of May 1979. Most of the people we contacted received us very positively. We did, however, experience a number of failures, such as with a very old woman who had agreed to meet us late one afternoon in the Bronx. Unaware of the distance and traffic problems, we were thirty minutes late before we had even gone a third of the way. We stopped to call her, but her son,

REMEMBRANCES

who seemed to be waiting for our call, answered the telephone with a very curt "Forget it!" and then hung up. In another case, a meeting with an elderly Sicilian man was canceled by his son without explanation on the day before filming, even though we had enjoyed very friendly contact with both of them eight days earlier. In these two cases, it seemed to us that the children did not want to see their parents dredge up these memories. In other cases, it was the subjects themselves who refused. One was an Italian barber in the Village, who had arrived at the age of sixteen, after World War I. He would have liked to tell us his story (which had already appeared in the Post in 1976 in a series of interviews on immigration for the Bicentennial), but he refused to be filmed. In another instance, the grandparents of a waitress in an Italian café in the Village, both of whom passed through Ellis Island, turned out to have come not from Italy as we had thought, but from Russia (him) and Poland (her).

In the end, two of the interviews we did could not be used either in the film or in this book:

LOUIE BALDUCCI
Owner of one of the finest grocery stores in New York—"One of the three best in the world," he assured us, the others being in Paris (Fauchon) and Milan—Mr. Balducci arrived from Bari in 1915, at the age of fifteen. He started out with a push cart, selling bananas in the streets of Brooklyn. His story—punctuated by trips to Italy (where his mother had insisted he return to marry), by false passports in the names of a brother or a cousin, by run-ins with the Italian authorities

106

(because he had not done his military service) or with Tammany Hall (the city of New York)—is completely typical of those immigrant families who arrived by the tens of thousands. But unfortunately for us, our interview with him turned out to be unusable. Not only because it took place in this very beautiful food store crowded with customers but above all because, contrary to what he had told us when we met with him the year before, Mr. Balducci emphatically refused to speak about Ellis Island, an island he said was reserved only for sick people and where, he insisted, he had never been.

THE THREE ITALIANS We made an attempt to interview three Italians in the basement of the Church of Our Lady of Pompeii, where lunch is served to parochial-school students and retired people from the neighborhood. They were Aniello Tufano, a life-long barber who arrived in 1923 at the age of twenty-three from a village near Naples; Antonio Mosca, born in 1892, who had arrived in 1910 from Sicily and had worked for many years as a sausage vendor at the races; and Giuseppe Piegari, who arrived in 1923 at the age of twenty-four and went to work on the railroads at Lake Erie. Naively, we had planned to have an "open" conversation in which the three interviewees would compare and contrast their memories and impressions. The inexperience of the interviewer (me) rendered this interview nearly indecipherable. It is likely these three interviewees never really understood what we expected of them.

MR. MORRIS MEROW

Born in Russia in 1909
Emigrated in 1921 at the age of twelve

REMEMBRANCES

We had met Mr. Merow the year before,
at YIVO, where we were introduced by Roselyn
Schwartz. At that time, we were planning
to do all our interviews on Ellis Island.
In fact, Mr. Merow and Mrs. Kakis were the only
interviewees to meet with us on the island.
The interview with Mr. Merow and his wife
took place on Thursday afternoon, May 10, 1979,
and began on the ferry.

Mr. and Mrs. Merow during the interview
with Georges Perec.

Next pages: The state of the ferry in 1979. It had
traveled over a million miles, shuttling between
the tip of Manhattan and Ellis Island; it carried
approximately a thousand passengers each time.

Georges Perec: Is this the first time you've come back
to Ellis Island?
Mrs. Merow: Yes, it's the first time he's been back.

GP: You've never been here?
Mr. Merow : She's never been before.
  (…)

GP: When did you emigrate to the United States?
Mr. M: I came here in 1921…in the middle
of the Russian Revolution.

GP: Where did you come from?
Mr. M: I was coming from Proskurov, and we left
almost immediately after the Proskurov pogrom.

GP: How old were you?
Mr. M: I think I must have been around twelve.

GP: Do you remember the trip?
Mr. M: We went through Anvers, in Belgium.

GP: Do you remember the boat's name?
Mr. M: It just came back to me…all of a sudden….
I think that the boat was called the *Samland*…
Samland…S.A.M.L.A.N.D.… The name stuck in my
head. I know that before we left, they told us the name
of the boats we were going to take…. But to get back to
the trip, I can assure you that I don't remember
it as some marvelous thing, except that I was going to
see my father for the first time…. I must have been two
or three years old when he left and I hardly knew him,
and during the war there was no communication
between Europe and the rest of the world. It was
blocked here and we were there. But as for the rest,
they told me, "you're going to arrive in the Land of
Liberty," but for me, that remained to be seen, because
in Kuzmin, where I lived until the age of five or six,
and then in Proskurov, the one thing I was taught was

not to trust anyone, least of all strangers. There was
a pogrom in Proskurov, organized by Pilsudski, and
I know that I lived in so much fear that it took many
weeks, even already being here, even having found
my father whom I hadn't had during the first part of my
life, to stop being frightened by the simple creak
of a door. When my father had me by the hand and we
walked through the streets the noise of a doorman
taking out the trash still made me jump....

(...)

In the baggage room

GP: Does this place remind you of anything?
Mrs. M: Do you remember anything?
Mr. M:...Yes...
Mrs. M: What do you remember, Morris? Was that
where you met your family?
Mr. M:...They had you go in here first...you had to
show your papers, say who you are, what you do...the
medical examinations...they checked all that....
I remember that it was my mother...may God keep her
soul, who had all the papers...

GP: How many were you?
Mr. M: There were three children...one sister older
than me and a little sister.... My mother had to show
lots of papers so that everything would be in order....
I remember there were a lot of people sitting and
waiting.... They sorted us, some went through the door
on the right and some through the door on the left....
I also remember that we were afraid they'd find
something on us, that we weren't clean. My mother
never forgot to check our heads to make sure they were
clean because at that time there weren't products
like there are today and it was normal for children to
get lice or things like that.

(...)

GP: How long was the trip?
Mr. M: Well, in fact, from Russia to here took us

a year.... We stopped in Warsaw, I don't remember exactly how long, but I remember it was so long that I thought I was in my new country.... There were all sorts of papers to fill out and doctors' appointments and we also had to wait for the boat, because the boat only took a certain number of passengers...

Mrs. M: Excuse me Morris, I want to ask you a question.... Were there a lot of people who were kept here because they were dirty, or did they let everyone leave?

Mr. M: At the time, as a child, I wasn't interested in figuring out who went through and who didn't, but I know that we left behind a lot of people we had met on the boat. There were a lot of people crying in each other's arms *(he is almost at the point of tears himself)*. I'm falling apart a little, excuse me. If the place had been kept up at all maybe I wouldn't feel so sad. This place is so sad now.... I remember that we were going into another room, and there were tables and booths, and they served you coffee. And everywhere you went, you were carrying everything you had. Every time you moved, you had to put all your bags on your shoulders, like a peasant, you know. I suppose we all seemed like peasants at the time, and I remember that I was thinking, after so many years, look at all a man owns: a bundle, some clothes in a bag, and a box on his shoulder.

(...)

GP: Do you remember the moment when your father came to get you?

Mr. M: I remember that my father came with one of his nephews, who must have been about fifteen years old at the time.... He took our things and we left.... Of course at that time, I had never seen a taxi.... We got into a taxi and we went to Brooklyn.... My father had an apartment there.... on the sixth floor, there was no elevator.... And looking back I can say that that's where my life started...in 1921 at twelve years old, because before, I don't think I appreciated life. I think that like many children in

Russia at that time, I would have preferred not to be born.

GP: When you were in Russia, did you talk about America?

Mr. M: With children my own age, I don't think so.... But I know that when my mother got the visas, lots of people envied us.... We were proud to be going to America even though it made us sad to leave all those people.

Mrs. M: He was torn between two emotions.

Mr. M: One of my uncles was killed in the Proskurov pogrom...he was still a very young man, but he had five children, the oldest must have been about eleven, and he also had an infant.... And two months later their mother died.... died of sadness.... And the family shared the children.... One of the little girls came to live with us...she was two or two-and-a-half years old, but when we left we had to leave her behind and it was like I had to abandon a sister.... And today she's planning to come to America and we're trying to help her.

GP: She's still in Russia.

Mr. M: She came to visit us eight years ago, and now she's trying to come here for good.

(...)

At the end of the visit

Mr. M: I remember the room where we waited before leaving.... That was where vendors could come in to sell ice cream or fruit or things like that and I distinctly remember asking my mother, "what is that?" She didn't know. It was a banana, but I didn't know until later, when I had to eat one...

GP: Do you remember your initial impressions, when you first explored New York?

Mr. M: Of course, at the time I didn't know that to go from Manhattan to Brooklyn, you had to cross a bridge. On the trip through Europe, I had seen marvelous things, things that awed me; for example, I remember the railroad station in Lemberg, which made a huge impression on me with its giant atrium. And of course, the bridge as well. Now I know that it was the Williamsburg Bridge.... It was very nice to be in that car with my brand-new father, and of course there was also the taxi driver. Later I understood that it was a taxi, but at the time I said to my mother, "How great! He came with his chauffeur!" And then we arrived at the house and less than a half-hour later the whole family knew that we were there. They started coming to see us and there was one cousin of mine, about my age, who said—they told me later—"You know, these greenhorns are really like us. They don't seem like greenhorns at all."

GP: Was he born in the United States?
Mr. M: Yes...and of course, I was old enough to go to school. It was certainly a year where there were lots of immigrants, because in my class there were many boys my age, and even older ones, who came from Poland and Ukraine and Russia, from everywhere. At the time, I spoke three languages: Yiddish, Ukrainian, and Russian, but I had to start over again from scratch, to learn my ABCs, in a class with the little ones... Little by little, we got used to it, we broke the language barrier....We found many relatives here that I didn't even know existed, and I made many friends.... And between my relatives and my friends, I think I've had a happy life, right up to this day when I'm sitting here next to my wife.... When I got married, in 1937, my parents invited I think 250 people.
Mrs. M: No, no, there were more than 300!
Mr. M: Yes, there were 300 guests at our wedding.... I'm not saying this to brag but just to show you how well we got along with people, because these weren't names we pulled out of a hat, these were people who knew us well and who we knew well; many were relatives and others were people who came from the same region in Russia that we did.... Many of them are dead now, but we could still get seventy-five or eighty together...

GP: Did you stay in touch with those who came from the same region in Russia as you?
Mr. M: Yes, and that's one of the things that is most precious to me. Everyone is proud of something exceptional in his life. Me, I'm proud of a promise that I made and that I continue to keep. My father had created a *Landsmanshaft** with members from every corner of the United States, not just New York but Chicago and the other states. Before he died he made me promise that I would continue that work and today that group is still functioning and my wife and I are actively involved in it (...)
There you go: I think that I've said everything I have to say. You've been very kind to me. You haven't contradicted me once! My wife, yes, but her I have to forgive....

GP: Thank you very much. It has been a great pleasure to meet you and we hope...
Mrs. M: that we see each other again.
Mr. M: We will see each other again and we hope that you will be rewarded for what you have done today, and I hope that I have helped you.

~

* Association of emigrants from the same town.

Mr. Baruch Chasimow

Arrived at the age of twenty-five in 1909

REMEMBRANCES

We met Mr. Chasimow through John Blum, a social historian at New York University who for several years has been collecting the oral testimony of early-twentieth-century American labor organizers. According to John Blum, Mr. Chasimow is blessed with a perfect memory—"total recall" of the demonstrations, meetings, and discussions in which he participated throughout his life. Even today, almost completely deaf, he speaks into the tape recorder with stunning ease and clarity, and when we asked him to do a sound check, he simply announced: "My name is Baruch Chasimow." Mr. Chasimow lives in the Bronx with his second daughter, but the interview took place in Manhattan at the home of his oldest daughter, on the afternoon of Thursday, May 17. At the end of the interview, he asked us to come back and see him in March of 1984, to celebrate his 100th birthday.

GP: When did you come to America?
Mr. Chasimow: I arrived here the fifth of May, 1909.

GP: How old were you?
Mr. C: I was born in 1884. Figure it out.... I was about twenty-five years old.

GP: Why did you leave Russia?
Mr. C: It was the old Russia, and I suffered a great deal from the persecution. I was arrested and put in jail many times.
In 1904, in Kursk, I was arrested for distributing a leaflet against the Russo-Japanese War. I stayed in prison close to eight months.
I also took part in the 1905 revolt. In the movement I was considered a good speaker and they asked me to talk at a workers' meeting in Kursk, which was a big industrial city. At that meeting I made an argument against the October Manifesto*; I explained that this Manifesto was nothing but a bluff, that we were going to be duped, that they weren't going to give us anything and that all these decrees, new laws, and the Constitution that they were pretending to give us wouldn't mean anything the next day and that the people would remain like before, in misery and oppression.

(During a part of the interview that we were not able to record, Mr. Chasimow told us that he was arrested again in 1906 and deported to Siberia, where he remained until escaping about two months later. He went to Kiev, and then to Odessa, where he got married—but he and his wife were arrested on their wedding day. He finally set off for America using his brother's passport.)

* Following the events of 1905, Nicholas II, advised by Witte, agreed to a legislative assembly (Douma) and published, in the Manifesto of 30 October, some liberal measures that were never applied.

REMEMBRANCES

GP: Did you have a family in America?

Mr. C: Pardon?

GP: When you arrived, was there family already here?

Mr. C: When did I become a communist?

GP: No. When you arrived here, did you have relatives? Brothers? Sisters?

Mr. C: Yes, I was the fifth in my family to come. There were nine of us altogether. There were seven children here in America. Only two are left today, a younger sister and myself.

GP: Do you remember your passage to Ellis Island?

Mr. C: When I arrived at Ellis Island, my older brother was supposed to wait for me and lead me out. There were a lot of people, herds, really, and the inspectors were pushing some to one side and others to another side. Nobody understood what was happening. Suddenly, I saw an inspector marking a cross on my sleeve. I was wearing a coat, a blue overcoat; I saw that on me he had made a cross, but on someone else, no cross, and they were pushing the ones with a cross to one side and the rest to the other. I didn't know why he had put this cross on me, so I took off my coat and I put it over my arm and I kept going.

GP: You didn't know what this cross meant?

Mr. C: No, I didn't know what it was. All I saw was that those with the cross went to one side and those with no cross went to another. And me, I preferred to go where those who didn't have a cross were going. I went there, found my brother, and he took me to his house.

GP: And that's all?

Mr. C: That's all. That same week, I got my identification papers and I found a job in Brownsville, near Brooklyn.

GP: You were in the garment business?

Mr. C: I worked in women's clothing, yes, and right away I joined the local ILGWU (International Ladies' Garment Workers Union). In 1910, I joined the general strike and I remember that Samuel Gompers came to speak to us at Madison Square Garden. At that time, Madison Square Garden was at 24th and Madison. It was very, very impressive. The president of the ILGWU at the time was a man by the name of Abraham Rosenberg, and the secretary was Lew Daitch. The strike lasted over ten weeks. Morris Hillquit was leading the meetings; there were also Meyer London and Jacob Panker. Just before the end of the strike, there was a coup organized against the leaders. A scab had been killed on Fourth Street and they were accused; but there were demonstrations at the trial and they were acquitted (…)

GP: What was your job?

Mr. C: I was in high fashion; I custom-made clothes for three big designers: Goodman, Carnegie, Millgram Brothers, or Stein and Blain. In 1915 we had the second big strike and one of the leaders betrayed us; he secretly negotiated with the owners and the union collapsed. At the end of the year, the union leaders approached me and said: "Chazenow"—my name in Yiddish is Chazenow—"you are the only one they trust, you have to try to reorganize the union." For six months, we went shop by shop and in 1916 the union was strong enough again to declare another strike and win a standard work week, with a minimum salary of $50.00 a week (…).

GP: You have always been very politically aware. When you came to America, during the crossing, what did you think of the immigrants?

Mr. C: I knew only that they were poor people, like me. I came from poor and I found poor. I knew that life was not going to be easier for us here, because the poor are poor and wherever they go, they won't get rich in one day. And the ones who are getting rich are doing it on the backs of the poor. It was the same thing when I went back to the USSR; I was not expecting to find Paradise, I knew that things would be hard there for a long time; but compared to what I had known, it was much better.

GP: Are you happy to have come to the United States? Do you think that it was a good thing for you?
Mr. C: Certainly at that time I was happy, because I had been all the time in prison. You know, I escaped from about three prisons. It was only when I was in prison in Kursk that I didn't try to escape, because I knew the whole town wanted to get me out of there; not just because I was young, but also because I was the first political prisoner in Kursk. When I got to the prison, the 1,500 or 1,700 prisoners there were all low-down criminals. They called me a Russian name that means the "nobleman," because I was wearing my own clothes; even the guards called me the "nobleman" because I asked for a pencil and paper to write with...

~

Mr. Baruch Chasimow in his Manhattan apartment.

MR. NATHAN SOLOMON

Emigrated in 1923

REMEMBRANCES

Nathan Solomon is the last of those we had met the year before, while we were scouting for locations. Like Morris Merow, he collaborates actively with Roselyn Schwartz's work at YIVO. Since his departure from Europe, he has kept an account of his life. During our first meeting, he read passages in Yiddish from the journal he has kept since he was held on Ellis Island. We would have very much liked for him to read again during our interview at his home on the afternoon of Monday, May 21, but it was not to be.

Mr. and Mrs. Solomon

Nathan Solomon: I was born into a middle-class family that was successful in business. We had a candy factory in the town of Sombor and we were three brothers and two sisters. To tell the truth, we were among the chosen families in town.

GP: The chosen?
NS: Yes, the chosen. I don't mean aristocrats, but the chosen, the minority of chosen. (…) I was born during the reign of the Austrian Emperor Francis Joseph. Then the empire was crushed…. In 1918 my father died in a sanitarium of tuberculosis. Then the Ukrainians came. Denikine, Petliura, it became impossible for the Jews. Impossible to live. We had never known pogroms, we had never been afraid for our lives. But after 1919, it was dangerous for a Jew to walk down the street. General Hall's men provided a taste of what was coming with Hitler. When they were in the street and they saw a Jew, a pious Jew with a beard, they took their bayonets and they cut his beard. I was young at the time, I was a student. I read Lenin and Trotsky but I was not interested in communism. I wanted to be a Jew above all things. Even in America, I remain the Jew that I always was.

GP: What were your studies?
NS: I have the papers here, I can show you. I studied accounting at the Handelsschule (business school) that was founded by the Jewish community. Then in 1921, I began work as a salesman for my family's business.

GP: Excuse me, you were the oldest son?
NS: No, I was the fourth. (…) I traveled the whole country and I saw a lot of people, Jews and non-Jews, but everywhere I went I encountered hate and anti-Semitism. And then in 1922 the first president of the Republic of Poland, Narutowicz, was assassinated, and the situation got very bad for the Jews. My mother, my brothers and my sisters, the whole family asked me not

to go, but I would rather be a hungry free man than a fortunate son with no freedom. I wanted to be free and freedom meant to go out into the world, to a free country, and there was no freer country than the United States. On June 6…June 26, 1923, I had decided to leave and the last words that I said to my mother at the railroad station were: "We are parting but I feel that I have the body and you have the soul." I left my mother, but I still carry the soul, until this day. And I arrived in Warsaw—I have the dates here— I had gotten my visa for the United States. On July 1, 1923, I left Warsaw for Danzig.

GP: Were you alone?
NS: Yes, I was alone. In fact, I had $1,000. My mother had given it to me and I carried it on my chest, under my shirt, in a little bag that she made for me.

GP: Do you still have the bag?
NS: Yes, I have it somewhere but I don't know where.… On July 3 we left Danzig for Cuxhaven* and there we got on the *Reliance.* It's all written here *(he presents a notebook with a black cover).*

GP: This is the journal you kept at the time?
NS: This is from Europe, yes. On July 11 we arrived in Cherbourg and on July 20 in New York. In New York they kept me…but for this I must go back a little… I refused to go serve in the Polish Army. I rejected it and I refused to do it. There was only one way to be declared unfit: I had to give myself trachoma.

GP: You gave yourself trachoma!
NS: I went to Doctor Yaworsky's house in Lemberg. He said: it's the only way. I had a friend who had trachoma. He gave me a piece of cotton, he rubbed his eyes with this cotton, and I rubbed my eyes in turn, and three days later, I had trachoma. The only thing

* A seaport in northwest Germany, at the mouth of the Elbe River.

was, arriving.… I had to go through a physical and it was enough to keep me. I had a paper from the Polish authorities to certify that I no longer had trachoma but they put me in the hospital on Ellis Island anyway. The first thing I did was make contact with the HIAS (Hebrew Immigrant Aid Society). They were on Lafayette Street at the time. They were very good to me, they told me not to worry and that they would take care of everything. But one day I spoke to the doctor— he turned out to be Jewish and spoke fluent Yiddish— and he said to me that my eyes were not healed. At the hospital, they were convinced that I had paid a Polish doctor to make up my certificate. And this doctor from Ellis Island said that he thought they would send me back. I was scared stiff.

GP: Scared stiff?
NS: Yes. I said to him immediately: "I shall not return to Poland. I shall only return as an American citizen. But I would rather jump in the sea than return to Poland as a Polish citizen." I wrote to the HIAS to tell them this, and a gentleman came to see me. I did not know who he was, but he asked my name and my birthday and this and that. He was very good to me, as if he had been my father. He was interested in what would happen to me. I asked someone who he was and I was told: that's Representative Dickstein, from New York, and he is going to intervene with the federal government on your behalf.… And finally they released me from Ellis Island. The HIAS told my cousins—of course I knew that I had relatives here, but I didn't know they had been informed of me—and the morning of July 25 they came to get me with my baggage. And we took the rail to South Ferry and they took me to Willett street to their apartment where they lived on the sixth floor. I had two little satchels with me, not with diamonds or anything, but with my underwear and my shirts. They walked with me up to the roof and they flung away the satchels and everything in them. Afterwards, I bought myself an outfit, everything I needed to dress like an American.

Nathan Solomon showing his passport to Georges Perec.

The journal that Nathan Solomon has kept since Ellis Island.

I looked like an American. And I was a free man. (…)

GP: Now let's talk about your life in America.
NS: With pleasure…I had the money from my mother, but I didn't want to use it and I started to look for work in the area I knew: candy. Only I respected the Sabbath and I did not want to go to work on the Sabbath. Finally I went to Luft, a non-Jewish company that had a candy factory, and I told them I was a confectioner, a European confectioner specializing in barley sugars, but that I did not want to work on the Sabbath. And they hired me anyway, and they said: "Stay home on the Sabbath. Have a good Sabbath." But then I had an accident. You can still see the scar. There (he shows us his finger). I was thinking about other things, and instead of putting the candy into the machine I put my finger instead. At that time there was no compensation. So I went three months with no work. I had a little money, but what hurt me the most is that I could not write to my mother and I knew that she was worrying. So I asked someone to write in my place that I had a little accident with my finger, and to prove to her that I was not desperate or short of money I sent her $250 (…) I did not want to continue doing nothing, so someone gave me the idea of selling newspapers. Each morning, at four

o'clock, I would go to buy the *Yiddische Morgenjournal*, which was the biggest of the Yiddish newspapers at the time....

I would buy twenty-five newspapers for forty cents, and I would go to Canal Street and Broadway, all around there, and I would call out, "*Morgenjournal! Morgenjournal!* Three cents!" I made thirty-five cents a day and that was enough to live on. It wasn't a lot of money, but it was enough. See, you went into a delicatessen and they gave you a good piece of bread and sausage for fifteen cents, and with a box of beans for twenty cents, it was almost too much.... (...)

And in 1925 I went into the butter-eggs-cheese business and opened a little shop. I worked very hard and at the end of four years I had five stores with the name *The New York Butter-and-Eggs-Stores* and my slogan was "Service with a smile!" My business was doing very well, and one day, in 1931, I went to my bank, CitiBank, at 53rd and Fifth by the Bay Bridge in Brooklyn—it was a Saturday morning, the banks were open on Saturdays at the time—and I deposited the money that I had made during the week in my stores. The bank manager approached me and said, "Mr. Solomon, I would like to talk with you." "With pleasure," I said. And then he said to me, "Why don't you invest your money? Do you know that you have a great deal of money here?" "How much?" I asked him. And he answered me "Your account is over ten thousand dollars." I said, "Are you sure there's no mistake? Maybe it's another Solomon. I have a cousin in Brooklyn, Barney Solomon." But told me "No, no. It's you, Nathan Solomon, we know you well." So when I was leaving I said to myself, "My mother deserves that I should go and visit her." Then there was the Wall Street Crash and people lost everything. But I, I had never bought any stocks, I had my money in the bank and there it was. So I took out my money and sold four of my five stores and I left for Europe on March 11, 1931.... (...)

When the Poles learned that I was there, a military inspector came to my mother and said "I hear that your son is here. We are looking for him because he has not done his military service." So then I said to him "Yes. I am here." And I showed him the American flag that I was wearing on my lapel, the emblem of American patriotism, and I said, "I have a passport right here. You and I no longer have anything in common. I am an American citizen, but you, you are Polish. I am here to see my mother. But you cannot do anything to me." And the next morning I got on the train to Lemberg and I went to the American consulate. I showed them my passport and I told them what had happened to me the day before. And the consul said to me, "Mr. Solomon, don't worry about anything. You are under my protection. You are a free American." And that was the happiest hour of my life.

～

MRS. ADLERSTEIN
Arrived in 1907 at the age of sixteen

MR. ZELDNER
Arrived in 1921 at the age of fourteen

REMEMBRANCES

Through a Parisian friend, we were introduced to Mrs. Fried, whose mother, Mrs. Adlerstein, had come to the United States in 1907 at the age of 16. The interview with Mrs. Adlerstein took place on the afternoon of May 22, in Mrs. Fried's house at Sea Gate, a residential development near the beach on Coney Island. Mrs. Fried and her husband were present, along with Max Zeldner, a cousin of Mrs. Adlerstein's who had come to the United States himself in June 1921, at the age of fourteen.

Mrs. Adlerstein.

Mrs. Adlerstein: What do you want to know? When did I come? I left Europe in 1900…
Mrs. Fried: and six.
Mrs. A: 1906. She knows better than I. I went to London.
GP: Where did you come from?
Mrs. A: I came from what they called White Russia.* If you want to know the exact name of the town where I lived with my parents, it was Slonim, in the province of Grodno…. But my three brothers were living in London, and later two of them went to the United States. After about a year, they had me come.

GP: They came for you on Ellis Island.
Mrs. A: Yes. It was not very difficult, because they were there and because I was coming from London and not from Russia.

GP: How old were you?
Mrs. A: I was sixteen.

GP: Did you speak English?
Mrs. A: Very little…. When I was in London, I wanted to study. But my brothers had very little money. They left Russia because they didn't want to go into the army of the Tsar. The oldest and the second went almost right away to the United States. The third was a young rabbi and he was about to get married. So I had to go to work.

GP: And what was your work?
Mrs. A: I was working in the clothing industry.
Mrs. F: That was in New York or London?
Mrs. A: In London.

GP: And did you also work in the dress industry in New York?

* Byelorussia.

REMEMBRANCES

Mrs. A: As soon as I arrived in New York, it was the same thing. My two brothers were still earning very little money. We all lived with an aunt, the sister of my mother....
I came on Sunday, and Tuesday I went to work (*laughter*).
Mrs. A: At the time, they were paying five dollars a week and my brothers said to me, "Five dollars. These days, that's a lot of money."

GP: What did your brothers do?
Mrs. A: The oldest had a little business. The other one was a mechanic. He worked with sewing machines.... The one who was in business did very well in the later years. But the other, the mechanic, he got very rich. He made knitting machines.

Max Zeldner: Ask her how old he is.
Mrs. A: Today, he is ninety-four years old.
    (...)

GP: Have you returned to Ellis Island?
Mrs. A: I returned to Ellis Island to fetch this cousin.
Max Z: Me.

GP: And what is your story?
Max Z: We also came from Europe. That was years later.

GP: Did you come from Russia?
Max Z: From Russia, too. It was Russia before World War I. It was Brest-Litovsk. The Germans came there in 1915, and everyone had to leave because it was a fortified city. They gave us three days to leave. My mother and my grandmother buried their valuables and we went to a little town, not too far from Slonim. Then there was the Russian Revolution in 1917, so as a little boy I had a chance to see the Bolsheviks. They came to town but they didn't stay long because Germans were coming. We remained there a few years until my father brought us over. He went to the United States before the war. He was a rabbi in Baltimore, Maryland. As a matter of fact, he sent for us during World War I, but the tickets were lost and he couldn't make enough money to send for us until 1921. That was when we left. We went to Danzig and from there to Liverpool and in Liverpool we boarded a boat called the *Coronia*. It was part of the Cunard Line, I believe. I don't remember how long it took, at least ten days or two weeks, but we arrived in June and while we were still on the boat Mrs. Adlerstein and her older brother Sam—the one who became so rich—and her husband and my father came by on a little boat and we waved to each other.

GP: How old were you in 1921?
Max Z: I was fourteen.
GP: Did you remember your father?
Max Z: I hadn't seen my father since I was about two years old. So when my mother said "That's your father," I said "Good, there's my father." (*laughs*.) I remembered him faintly, you see. I had known that he had a beard and he was bald, and he still had a beard and he was still bald (*laughter*), even though he had a hat. I was really very overjoyed to see this family coming to meet us on the little boat.... We stayed on Ellis Island a very short time, and I think...it was there I was given the name of Max... a German name, because my Hebrew name was Mordechai, from the Book of Esther. That's all I remember about Ellis Island. After, when we got to solid ground, they took us to Brooklyn, to Mrs. Adlerstein's brother's house. That was the first time I saw an American house, a very nice house, clean, orderly. And then my father, my mother, my grandmother, and I went to Baltimore, where my father had an apartment next to the synagogue, and that's where I began my life in the United States. I went to grammar school. I was much older than the other children in my class, but I learned English quickly, so my father sent me to New York to learn Hebrew, and later I went to Columbia University. I earned my living

Mr. Zeldner.

teaching Hebrew in a school. At the time I was earning twenty-five dollars a week, which made me almost a rich man. Then my father became a rabbi in Boston and I went to Harvard to continue my studies. I returned to Columbia to get my doctorate, then went into teaching and now I'm the head of the Department of Foreign Languages in a teachers' school. I direct language instruction in French, German, Spanish, but also Latin, Hebrew, and even Swahili (*laughter*).

(...)

GP: (to Mrs. Adlerstein)
Do you remember your life in Russia?
Mrs. A: We were nine children. My father had a mill.
Mrs. F: A flour mill.
Mrs. A: My father made flour and my mother had a store where she sold it.
They made a living but they were not rich. I would have liked to study and go to *Yeshivah* (Jewish university), but you had to pay for that, and my parents could not. I thought that the best thing for me was to go and find my brothers in London and I started begging my parents to let me leave. When my brother the rabbi got married, my father agreed to let me go. He wanted to go to London with me for the wedding. But he could not leave his work just like that, so I went by myself. I thought that my brothers would send me to study, but I had to start working right away. Here, it was the same thing. I went to school at night, but it was really hard for me, after working a whole day. Because at the time, people didn't have electric machines like they do now. Everything was with the feet. And it was so strict, you were not allowed to speak. If you needed something for the machine, you weren't allowed to pick up your head and say so, because that would waste time. You had to do this (*she strikes the arm of her chair with her fist*) by the machine and someone came. It was often necessary to work Saturday and sometimes, when it was very busy, you had to go in on Sunday.
Later, I met a young man and we became engaged.

We started making sweaters by machine and we opened a store. And as soon as we saw that the store allowed us to earn a living, we got married. Just a few years later I stopped working and I was able to ask my friend's son, who was a teacher, to come and give me lessons.

(...)

GP: (To Mrs. Fried)
Do you have photographs of your family in Russia?
Mrs. F: Yes, I do. This is a picture of my mother's family.... It was taken just before she left for London. This is the rest of her family, her mother, her father, her four sisters, and her brother....
The three other brothers were already in London. She's the only one of the sisters who left home.

GP: The others did not come to America.
Mrs. F: Only one of them came after the war. She survived the Holocaust. All the others are dead....
Here's a picture of my brother's wedding in London. This is my mother, and this is the groom, the rabbi, the one who stayed in England.
Max Z: Tell him.
Mrs. F: Oh, later, in good time.

GP: What does he want you to tell me?
Mrs. F: It's about the rabbi. He has a son who was made a Lord. He's a very successful lawyer, and at one point he was president of the London County Council; he was also the director of the National Theatre. So that's how we have a Lord in the family.

Mrs. Adlerstein interrupts her daughter to show us another photograph.

Mrs. A: This is my sister with her husband and their two children. That's me and that's a younger sister, and that's a brother. My brother was married after I left and had two children, and here is the only sister that was saved from Hitler. This one and this one and this one and all the children were...

REMEMBRANCES

GP: And the one who survived is the one who came here after the war. (…)

GP: (to Mrs. Fried) Have you been back to Europe with your mother?

Mrs. F: We went there to see my family in 1923. It was for my aunt's wedding. My uncle came from London and my mother came with me. We were just staying for a short time, for the wedding, but my mother didn't want to go back right away; she wanted to be with her family, and in fact we ended up staying all winter and until spring. We didn't come back to the United States until June.

GP: Do you have memories of the trip?

Mrs. F: I remember very well…
I was nine years old at the time.…
It was completely different from everything I knew. The first thing I remember is that they didn't have indoor bathrooms (*laughter*). It took me a week to get used to it. And of course, no one spoke English. I knew very little Yiddish, but in a short time I learned to speak fairly well, and I also learned Russian. By the time I left I even spoke a little Polish. I also took some piano lessons.
For me it was a wonderful thing, because when I read stories about the *shtetl* today I know what they're talking about.… Come Friday night, or Saturday, you knew it was Shabbas because there were no sounds of any kind. Everything was still, all the lights were out, only the candles were flickering, nobody did anything, nobody thought to do anything. I will always be grateful to my mother for having me take that trip, because not only was I able to meet my mother's family but I was able to have this experience.

～

MR. SEMYON SHIMIN

Born in Astrakhan (Russia) in November 1902
Arrived in America in June 1912

REMEMBRANCES

We met Semyon Shimin, painter and illustrator of children's books, through Robert Bober's English teacher.
The interview took place in his studio on the morning of Wednesday, May 23.

GP: Do you remember your arrival in America?
Semyon Shimin: Oh, it was a very hot day, in June 1912.

GP: Do you have memories of Russia?
SS: Yes, some…from the age of about five…I had no schooling there, just at the *Heder*, the Hebrew school…. I was a very mischievous boy…. I remember that I loved music, I wanted to be a musician, maybe because in my family there was one uncle who was a composer…and there were always a lot of musicians in our house…. Of course, I also remember my excitement the day I was told we might be leaving for America…They had told us all sorts of stories about America, we got letters in which they told us that America was the country where everyone had a chance…

GP: How many people were in your family?
SS: There were six of us including my parents…. There was a baby, a little girl…
Sadly, she came down with pneumonia on the boat and died two months after we arrived….
I also remember that we had many friends in Russia, people of all nationalities…. There were the Tartars, the Persians, the Russians, the Jews…. I liked to do sculpture, but I didn't draw….

GP: Do you remember the trip?
SS: Yes, I think that it took us about two weeks to cross Russia. We took the boat from Libava,* which is in Estonia, I think. And from there, it took two more weeks to get to New York. I remember very clearly that we were very nervous, because it was just after the sinking of the *Titanic** and everyone on the boat was a little afraid.

Mr. Semyon Shimin.

* Liepaja. In German, Libau.
* April 15, 1912.

131

REMEMBRANCES

GP: Were you in steerage?

SS: I don't know, I don't remember very well. The pictures I've seen of immigrants in steerage are very different from the memories I have. It certainly wasn't first class....

In any case, what I do remember is that I spent most of my time on deck. I loved to look at the ocean. It was very beautiful weather.... (...)

I'd like to back up a little...

In the summer, in Astrakhan, Mama took the whole family up the Volga. We went upstream for an entire month.... She had sisters living in Kazan, in Nijni-Novgorod....

GP: What did your father do?

SS: He was a cabinet maker. He had an antique store full of wonderful things, icons, antiques, stuffed animals.(...)

GP: Do you remember Ellis Island?

SS: I only remember that we disembarked somewhere that looked like a boat, but wasn't a boat...a big building with a lot of people where they were checking papers...but I don't remember the medical exams or anything like that.... In fact, I don't have visual memories, except of the crowd surrounding me....

I don't think we were there more than two hours.

GP: Did you have relatives in the United States?

SS: It was thanks to them that we came.... My father's brothers didn't want to do their service in the Tsarist armies, so they had left many years before.

Then my grandmother came, then all of us.

They lived on the East Side. That's where we stayed when we first arrived.... But it wasn't long before the situation became serious and a little sad. Father was petrified by what he saw in New York, by the crowds.... He understood that it was out of the question to open another antique store.... He didn't have the finances for that...after about two months, he took on a small delicatessen in Brooklyn....

In the back of the store there were two little rooms and all of us lived there. It was a big change for us from the very, very large place that we had in Astrakhan. Father's feeling was that this was all wrong, that we were going backwards, but I thought this promised to be quite interesting...

GP: Did you go to school?

SS: I was nine years old, but they put me with the youngest children. I was very unhappy. The boys from the higher grades made fun of me. But the teacher was very kind to me; she gave up part of her lunch hour to work with me.

And almost every month I went up a grade, to catch up with my age group. I was a good student. I wanted to learn. When I was ten years old, I decided that I wanted to be an artist. Originally I had wanted to be a musician, like my uncle the composer. But he said, "No. Certainly not!"

GP: He lived in America?

SS: He came when my father's other brothers did, yes, but his career as a composer had been a failure, and he didn't want another failure in the family.

I don't know how it happened, but in the ten days that followed, not even two weeks later, I started drawing. (...) At fifteen, I began working as an apprentice with a graphic designer. In three years, I learned everything I needed to learn. From that moment on, I was independent. I worked every night to make a living, but during the day I painted.... My first years here were very difficult.... We lived in a very poor neighborhood and my mother worked under very difficult conditions.... Domestic work.... I would bring her sweaters, bundles of sweaters, and she would sew the buttons on, for a few cents...(...)

GP: You never returned to Russia?

SS: No. Never. I would like to.

GP: Do you have any family there now?

REMEMBRANCES

SS: I don't think so. The last thing I heard was
in a letter that came from Geneva: someone who had
seen a reproduction of one of my paintings and
said we were relatives. He had left Russia during the
war and moved to Switzerland. My mother's family
is completely dispersed, my father's is all here.

Georges Perec and Semyon Shimin.

~

MRS. SCHWARTZ

Arrived from Russia in January of 1921,
at the age of twenty-one

REMEMBRANCES

Mrs. Rose Schwartz is not related to Mrs. Roselyn Schwartz, who introduced us to her. The interview took place at Mrs. Schwartz's home in the Bronx on the morning of May 25—a fact she felt compelled to indicate at the beginning of the taping, instinctively obeying a rule of interviews for American television.

GP: Where are you from?

Mrs. Schwartz: Today is May 25, 1979. I come from Kishinev, the capital of Bessarabia. At the time it was part of Russia. I was born on July 31, 1900.

GP: So you are seventy-nine years old?

Mrs. S: Soon I will be…. We lived in Tsarist Russia at the time. Then came World War I. Two of my brothers fought. I had a sister who lived in Paris with her family and another one who lived in a village in Bessarabia. My parents died during the war. In 1917 there was the socialist revolution, and in a way we were very happy because we had been oppressed and we had lived through so many pogroms. But a little later, Bessarabia was annexed by fascist Romania. Bessarabia was a fertile country; no one ever went hungry, there was plenty of wheat, there were vegetables and fruits. But the Romanians took it all from us. We couldn't even find a real piece of good bread any more—only a sort of yellow flour. We were truly starving, there was no work, we didn't have the right to go out at night, and as soon as there were two or three people talking together in the street they were arrested right away and beaten horribly. Many young people left Bessarabia. I left Kishinev, I went to the village where my sister lived, and I met a young man who fell in love with me. We were married on my birthday, July 31, 1918. And the following year I had a daughter. My husband was a men's tailor but it was really impossible for us to live. We were scared of everything and we were starving. My husband had two brothers in America and he said to me, "I have their address. They have already written me letters. They work there, they earn a living, they are free. I want to go to America. We are both young—let's go." We sold all our furniture, everything we owned, my husband's sewing machine, everything, and we took a boat to Galatzi. There was water in the hold and we had an awful journey. Then we made a stop and they told us to

REMEMBRANCES

get off the boat and go into quarantine. We were forced to undress and to give our clothes up to be sterilized…

GP: You don't remember at which port this happened? Mrs. S: No, I think it was Greece or Italy…in any case, it was really horrible.… Afterwards we arrived at Le Havre, and we took the train to Paris from there. I had my sister's address but I hadn't been able to write to tell her we were coming. We took a taxi and when we arrived at my sister's, the driver came with us and told her, "You have some visitors." My sister looked at me and asked, "Who are you?" When she had left me I had only been ten years old and now I was twenty, married, and with a one-year-old daughter. My brother-in-law and my sister did not want me to go to America. They had a shop in Paris, they earned a good living and they offered to help us if we stayed with them in France. But my husband said, "No. I've heard so much about America, I have read all of the books Karl Marx wrote about it: you can find work, and the workers live better and are free. We have to go see it with our own eyes." We didn't have enough money so we sent a telegram to my husband's brothers so they would send us tickets for the boat—two tickets for us and a half-fare for the baby. They only sent him $200, but my brother-in-law and my sister also loaned us some money and we were able to take the least expensive boat there was. It was a troop carrier, for American soldiers going home after the war. This was its last trip, they destroyed it afterwards. There were just two big cabins; one for men and one for women. And there was nothing to eat but potatoes and herring. They gave us milk for the baby. It took us twenty-one days to come to America—you can imagine the conditions! Well, when we landed we expected to find a different world, but all we found was Ellis Island—a large room with steel bars on the windows, a prison. It was a terrible disappointment for us—this was the beautiful America. There weren't even chairs or benches to sit on, everyone sat on the floor, in the filth! After such a hard

trip, we thought we had left behind the old Russia of the tsars and the Romania of the fascists; we were hoping to find someplace warm, someplace clean. But instead, we had bars on the windows and were forced to sit on the floor. We had to wait for the doctors to call us in for a medical examination. With my baby and myself there was no problem. But they were very worried about my husband's eyes. At the time there was a disease called trachoma. So they sent him to another room to be examined by another doctor. It took about an hour and I was very unhappy, waiting for him; I was afraid they would send him back. In the end everything worked out, and we took the boat to go to New York, where my husband's two brothers were waiting for us. This was in January of 1921. It was very, very cold. We weren't dressed warmly enough. We stayed with one of my brothers-in-law, who was married and had a daughter, in an apartment in the Bronx across from the zoo, an apartment with four tiny rooms where the three of us slept in one small bed.
I got sick and my daughter got sick almost at the same time. I couldn't take care of her and she went to a city hospital where they completely neglected her. In the meantime, my husband found a job right away. It was downtown in a women's dress shop, a rotten place with no elevator, just a lift that you worked yourself by pulling on the ropes. We managed to find an apartment, which was a very hard thing to do back then. There was no electricity and no bathtub, but at least my husband had work and we had a place to live. I wanted to bring my baby home but the doctors said she was too sick; after nine weeks, I lost my baby.
I would have liked to have gone to work but my husband didn't want me to, so I started to work for the unions. Back then, workers had to struggle very hard because they worked ten hours a day and six days a week, and when the boss needed you on Sunday you had to go in or you lost your job. I had a son at that time, God bless him, and it was very, very, very hard. The worker labored so hard that he couldn't even see his children. He never had the pleasure of talking or

REMEMBRANCES

playing with his child. We have a Jewish writer, Avrom Reisen, who wrote a song about the American worker. Do you want me to sing it to you in Yiddish?

*Mrs. Schwartz recites in Yiddish**

My little child

I have a little child
A little boy so pure
That I think, as I look at him,
That the whole world belongs to me

But I see him rarely, rarely,
when my beautiful boy is waking
I always see him asleep
Because I only see him at night

Work takes me away from home so early
and frees me so late at night
Oh, my own flesh is foreign to me
foreign is my son's gaze.

I come home exhausted
Enveloped in darkness
My poor wife eagerly tells me
How happily our child plays

How his voice is soft and his spirit lively
"Oh Mama, my good Mama,
When he comes home, he will bring me a penny
My Papa, my good Papa!"

I hear it and I hurry
Ah yes, this must happen
My love as a father illuminates me
I have to see my child

I keep close to his cradle
I see him, I listen, I am quiet
A dream makes his lips tremble
"Where is he, where is my Papa?"

I look at his little blue eyes
That open, Oh, my child
They see me, they see me
And then close again right away.
   (...)
I am full of pain and weariness
Filled with bitterness, and I think:
When you awaken, my child,
You will not find me anymore.

Mrs. S: There were so many strikes. Once my husband was on strike for twenty-six weeks! And there were no unemployment benefits back then. You had to fight for everything, for fewer hours, for better pay, for better working conditions because the shops were horrible and of course today workers live better and New York is no longer the city that it once was. Now it's the most beautiful city in the world...(...)

~

* In fact, this poem is not by Avrom Reisen, but by a writer who came before him, Morris Rosenfeld.
Born in 1862 in Poland, Rosenfeld arrived in New York in 1882 and worked as a tailor until his death in 1923.
His poetry, essentially social criticism, describes the poor conditions of workers in the sweatshops.

MR. CHAIM LIPA RUBMAN

Born in Poland in 1896
Immigrated in 1928

REMEMBRANCES

On Thursday, April 26, a ceremony called "Ellis Island Revisited" was held to honor the presence of Isaac Bashevis Singer on Ellis Island. After the usual speeches, the 400 Jews who had gathered there assembled before a huge American flag, breaking with equal fervor into both the Israeli and American anthems. It was on that day that we met Chaim Lipa Rubman. Mr. Rubman was born in 1896 in Radom, like Robert Bober's father. He was so happy to meet someone from his native city that he insisted on speaking to the film crew in Yiddish. This meeting presented the excuse for the interview, which took place late in the afternoon on Wednesday, May 30th, at the Bronx home of Mr. Rubman's youngest son, George. Gathered around the family table were Mr. Rubman, his two sons, his two daughters-in-law and two of his granddaughters. With three generations together this way, the interview also touched on the feelings that each had of immigration and of their roots in the American nation. This conversation alternated between Yiddish* and English.

* in italics in the text.

Robert Bober: *Why did you leave Radom for Israel and then go to New York?*
Mr. Rubman: *The Polish government wanted to take me into the army so I told them* (he sings in Polish and tells us the gist of the song):
I did not come here to put on a uniform so the Poles can say to me "Jew, dirty Jew!" This I did not want. I got rid of everything, I put on old clothes and I got help in leaving. I traveled alone to Kraków and from there I was given fake papers for Vienna, Austria. From Austria I went to Italy. The Italians gave me food. I worked on a boat to eat. Then I arrived in Port Said, and from there I went to Palestine.

Carl: That's where I was born.

GP: And you, were you born in Poland?
George: I was born in Poland.... We are a family that travels.

GP: And your father was born in Radom?
George: In Radom. And our mother was born in Radom, too.

GP: And they went to Israel first?
George: Yes, one after the other. They were married in Israel...

GP: And they returned to Poland?
Carl: My father had a visa to come to the United States. But alone. My mother did not have a visa...

GP: Why didn't your mother have a visa?
Carl: Why? Because there was a quota... I think.
George: They only approved a visa for Dad.
Carl: Yes, he was the only one who got a visa. So my mother and I went to Radom—my mother was pregnant with George at the time.

REMEMBRANCES

GP: To Radom? You went back to Radom?
Carl: Yes. Then George was born there, and two years after my father came to the United States, we came, too.

GP: Do you have memories, do you remember Radom?
Carl: Radom? Yes, I remember certain things.

GP: How old were you?
Carl: Oh, I was there from four years old to about seven. I remember my father's father, where he lived just outside the city. And the bakery that belonged to my father's family....
And that's about it.
(laughter)

GP: And when the two of you came to America with your mother, did you go through Ellis Island?
George: No, I think Ellis Island was closed when we arrived.

GP: When was that?
George: We came in 1930.

GP: Oh yes, it was closed. Ellis Island was closed in 1924. And I suppose all the immigration papers were filled out by your father?
George: Yes, my father sponsored my mother, my brother, and myself.

RB to Mr. R: *And you? Did you go through Ellis Island?*
Mr. R.: *I was supposed to go through Ellis Island. When I arrived in Providence, Rhode Island, I said, "I want to see the Statue of Liberty, but from the inside, not the outside." They said, "All right, do you have some money?" I had only a few Italian nickels.*

George and Carl: Italian nickels? Lire.
Mr. R: Yes, nickels or lire or whatever you want to call them. So they said, "Well, you can't go in without

money. What else do you have?" I said, "Nothing, a pillowcase, I only have a pillowcase." "And what kind of trade do you know?" So I said to him, "Masonry, bricklaying, etc." Fine, we're going to call the Jewish organization.
GP: HIAS?
Mr. R: Yes, HIAS. Someone from the organization gave me a piece of paper saying that I had come through Ellis Island and they said: "Go home now. Everything is O.K."

Mr. R turns toward RB: *If you want to ask me why I departed from Russia, from Poland, I will tell you one thing: (he sings some lines from L'Internationale). I left because my hunger was great, The filth was terrible, and I did not want to be constantly humiliated. So I said, "Hey Chaim Lipa—my name is Chaim Lipa—out! Get out of here."*
    (...)

RB: *I would like to know what you did here. How did you make your living when you first came to America?*
Mr. R: *Bricklayer, mason...and my boys learned to do the same thing. They went to high school and when they got out, they saw and I saw too that it would be just as well to have them work with me.*

George: At first my father worked as a mason, and after the war my brother and I joined our father and started a business that has done well, that we still run today. He's still very active today.

GP: He's still active?

George: He still works very hard.
(he pats his father on the back gently)
Julie: He still climbs up roofs every day.

RB: *Were you doing that kind of work in Poland?*
Mr. R: *In Poland, I worked in leather. I worked in a*

REMEMBRANCES

Mr. Chaim Rubman and his son George.

tannery. I made good leather. I prepared it to make shoes and boots. You know already!

(…)

(*Rubman shows photographs.*)

RB: *Is that your father?*
Mr. R: *My father, yes.*

RB: *What did he do?*

Mr. R: *What all fathers do—he worked hard for his children. He had seven, eight children, he worked hard on the railroad, he unloaded the box cars and brought sugar, salt, pepper, flour, and other things to the city. That way the children more or less had something to live on.*

GP: How many children did he have?
Mr. R: Eight.

Mr. Chaim Rubman and some of his family.

GP: And how many came to America?

George: Ida, Charlie, Max, and my father. Four here and another in Argentina. The others stayed in Europe and they…

Mr. R: I am the only one still alive.

George: Now he is the only one…the only one.

Mr. R: That's the way the world is, you know…

it turns, turns, turns…with no end.

George: It changes speeds. It's okay…

   (…)

GP: (*In French, to Julie*): I would like to ask you, not just you, but also your parents and your sister, how the immigrant experience has touched you personally.

REMEMBRANCES

For example, do you see a connection between the fact that your grandfather came from Radom, giving up everything to come live in America, and the present state of mobility of American families? Or is this for you more characteristic of the Jewish tradition?
Shirley: I see this diaspora as a part of the American experience. Most of the people we know have similar stories.
Ellen: Grandpa would like to keep everyone right here, in the Bronx. And yet when he was young he left Poland for Israel and left his family and came to America. And now my sister is in Boston, another cousin is in Washington. He would love for everyone to come back to the Bronx. He doesn't want anyone to leave home.
George: It's just the continuation, as Ellen says, of my parents leaving their roots, their place, their family. And I am sure that their families looked at them the same way we look at our children when they go to Boston or California or Washington. There are many reasons why people leave home, and experience the mobility you describe. Fifty or sixty years ago the problems were persecution and the difficulty of earning a living. These days there are more opportunities for young people in other parts of the country, and we carry on the same tradition, really, as my father and mother when they left Europe to come here. What they were looking for and found in the United States was a comfortable, safe place to raise their family. If they hadn't found that, I'm sure nothing would have kept them here.

GP: Yes, but at the same time you have memories of the country you're leaving. All the photographs on the table suggest your roots may be elsewhere. I don't know how you feel, but I suppose that you consider yourself American.
George: My roots are here, and they're here because my family is here. And if my family decided, or if the children decided to go elsewhere, I would consider if it was possible for me to go there as well. We're used to mobility today. It's nothing to take a plane—in seven or eight hours you're 6,000 miles away. It's O.K. for a trip, but I would never think of leaving here permanently. I have found it a very comfortable place to live. That said, I would be happy to go to Paris for a visit once in a while (*laughter*).

(…)

Julie: Personally, what stays with me are the stories that I hear. That's what I know about Poland, it's what I know about my grandfather's life, and my grandmother's life, and my other grandfather's (*he was from Poland also*). And we remember it and try to appreciate how they struggled and why they ran away. The best we can do is remember and call it a part of our past and a part of our roots. But our experience is here.

~

MRS. KAKIS

Born in Italy in 1911

Emigrated for the first time in 1912, returned to Italy in 1920,
and emigrated again in 1924

REMEMBRANCES

A number of times, taking the first ferry of the morning from Battery Park to Ellis Island, we met architects who were working on the restoration of the buildings. This is how we learned that one of their mothers-in-law, Mrs. Kakis, had been detained at Ellis Island for more than two months. She agreed to return with us. The interview took place on the island late on the morning of Thursday, May 31.

Mrs. Kakis' story is quite complicated, and interview conditions forced us to simplify it. Actually, Mrs. Kakis came to America for the first time at the age of one-and-a-half in 1912. Like many Italians at the time, the family returned to its native country in 1920 but had to emigrate once again in 1924, at a time when the conditions for entry into the United States had become considerably stricter.

Georges Perec and Mrs. Kakis.

Near the landing, in front of the entrance to the buildings

GP: I'll let you look first.

Mrs. Kakis: Yes, it's this one. Let me see. This is going to bring back memories. I'm happy to come back here, but the memories that I have are memories of a hard time. (…) My father was already here when I came the first time. I don't remember. I was one-and-a-half years old. I came with my mother and my older sister. We stayed for about ten years. My four brothers and sisters were born here. And in 1920, we went back to Italy. My father had earned some money and my grandmother was by herself over there, and she wrote us that she had a lot of land. So my father thought he had saved enough money for us to return there and work. But, you know, one year, two years passed. The money ran out. With six children, we didn't have much to eat. So my mother said, "We have to go back." But my father wanted to stay, he said, "No, no next year we will grow more olives. We will make back the money." But when the money never came, my mother said, "Listen, we must do something." They went to Rome, to the consulate, and my mother told them it was very difficult for her to live in Italy with six children after having lived in the United States for so long. So six months later the consul wrote my parents that it was all right and that we could go on the *Providence.*

GP: That was the name of the boat?
Mrs. K: Yes…but when we got here we weren't allowed to come back in.

GP: Your father was not an American citizen?

Mrs. K: Yes, that's why. And my mother got sick. She started spitting up blood and they put her in the hospital. They split us up. You know, we couldn't even go see her.(…)

REMEMBRANCES

In the baggage room

Mrs. K: It was like the rec room.... You know, it was a big room like this one. We sat, they brought us little things to make so we were entertained.... It really looks haunted now, with nobody in it, you know, because it used to be filled with a lot of people...yes, I can see it.... It's really dilapidated now, it was tidier then, but now it all looks broken down....
Yes, I remember it clearly.(...)

In the main room

Mrs. K: Every day they called the names here.... Sometimes they called the ones who had to go back and sometimes they called the ones who had the right to enter into the United States. But we were here every day and we never heard our name called. It was hard. And while my mother was in the hospital, my little brother got sick. Every morning a doctor and a nurse came to check our temperatures and one day they found him with a fever. So right away they said, "He's sick, we have to take him to the hospital," but I told them, "No, no, he's not sick, it's just because our mother isn't here." But right away they took him to the hospital and there he got double pneumonia...

GP: But four of your brothers and sisters were born in America?
Mrs. K: Yes. All four.

GP: They were American citizens?
Mrs. K: Of course. It's because of that that we finally won. Because when they saw that we weren't being allowed back in, my parents' friends got a lawyer, a big-time lawyer. He came to Ellis Island and asked my mother, "You never bought a house, you never bought any property in the United States?" And my mother said, "No, the only thing that I have in the United States is another little boy that died, and I have a plot in the cemetery." "Oh," he said, "but that's something;

I'll see what I can do with that." He left us and he studied the case with other lawyers. He came back at the end of a week and said to us, "Well, it looks like maybe we'll win the case because of that. You don't own a house but you are a property owner. It's a plot of land that belongs to you." And it's because of that that we got to leave—but not the four kids. To the kids who were born here they said, "We're happy to let you come in because you have the right to come in." But my mother, my father, my sister, and me, we were born in Italy and we didn't have the right to come in. So my mother said, "But who's going to take care of them? We don't have anybody in the United States."
It was a very difficult thing, she couldn't leave her children. Well, the lawyers worked on the case and we finally won. But we stayed on the island for several weeks, without my mother, and we couldn't even see each other. My sister and I were with my two little sisters and my father and my brother were with the men. You know, they didn't allow men and women to be together. Only an hour a day, for lunch. Right after lunch the guard would say, "You, go over here, and you, go over there.(...)"

In the dining room

GP: Do you remember this dining hall?
Mrs. K: Of course. But there were a lot of tables, you know. Now it's empty. There were tables everywhere. You would go get your own dish, there weren't any waitresses to serve you, and over there was this sort of little table with dishes and they would give you food and then you went to sit and eat. Not that the food was very good, but we ate.

GP: What kind of food did they give you?
Mrs. K: Potatoes, a lot of potatoes, not much meat. Sometimes stew. You know, stew—oh yes, stew, we had that about four times a week. On Sundays they gave us chicken.

REMEMBRANCES

GP: Do you remember these windows?

Mrs. K: I remember, yes. It was the only place we could look out. We couldn't go outside, you know, not even to get some fresh air or see the light. Only through these windows. We weren't allowed in the yard…(…) When they let us leave, we were happy, I can tell you that…. Every day, every day we cried. Every day we saw people leaving, but not us. People would stay one day, two days, and then they could go. But we never got called. Every time they would come for the roll call and they called those who could leave and they didn't call us, my mother would start crying and crying and crying. But then when they did call us, we couldn't believe it; we took a couple of the suitcases and we had to come back for the trunks a week later. But my mother still came back every day to see her baby. Because when we were here, we could only see him once a week. But when they let us into America, a nice Italian doctor said we could come back and see him every day. Because no one took care of him. He only had a little fever, maybe a cold, but they put him under a cold shower and he got a double pneumonia. They didn't even take care of him. He was there like a guinea pig. The nurses could not have cared less….

(…)

GP: You've never returned to Italy since?

Mrs. K: No. Not since 1924. My father had a good job. He made artificially flavored ice cream. My mother worked at home. And at about fifteen or sixteen, I began to sew…. I wasn't paid much, but if you made the whole dress yourself you could get by. Because often, there were some who worked as in an assembly line, one made the collar, one made the sleeve, etc. But if you made the whole dress you got paid a little more. That went on for years and years and then I met my husband and we got married.

GP: What kind of work did he do?

Mrs. K: He was a chef.

GP: Chef? Cook?

Mrs. K: Yes, head cook. He worked in a French restaurant and then in the Commodore Hotel. Then at the 60th East Club…for high society people. (…)

~

MRS. GASPERETTI

REMEMBRANCES

We interviewed Mrs. Gasperetti early in the afternoon on Thursday, May 31, 1979. The interview took place in the small game room of a senior citizen's center in Greenwich Village. Mrs. Gasperetti was accompanied by three of her friends. Behind her, a number of elderly Italians were playing cards. At the sound of the slate, Mrs. Gasperetti exclaimed, "Oh! Take one! Take one! Just like the movies."

GP: Mrs. Gasperetti, you were very young when you came to the United States. How old were you?
Mrs. Gasperetti: I was eighteen...well, not quite, but let's say eighteen.

GP: What year was that?
Mrs. G: 1912

GP: So you're eighty-five now?
Mrs. G: Yes.

GP: Did you come from Italy?
Mrs. G: Yes.

GP: What part of Italy?
Mrs. G: The province of Pavia. Paese Gombolo, a village in the Pavia region.

GP: Why did you leave for America?
Mrs. G: Well, I had three sisters here, so you know how it can be; I didn't want to leave my mother, and when my sister came back and wanted to bring me here I said no, I said, "I don't want to leave Mother alone here." And then all of a sudden I changed my mind. You know, everyone always goes to America for the same reason: the almighty dollar.

GP: To earn money, to become rich. Were your sisters rich?
Mrs. G: Oh no, not rich. My father was a tailor and a tailor is never really rich. Anyway, we were four sisters and we all came here, one after the other, and my brother too, my only brother. I am the only one left. They're all dead.

GP: You were the last one to come over?
Mrs. G: I was the last of the family and I am the last, I am the only one left, yes...

REMEMBRANCES

GP: Where did you catch the boat? In Genoa?

Mrs. G: Yes. And I got to the United States on February 22. Washington's birthday. When I saw the Statue of Liberty for the first time, I was truly impressed. Oh, I was so happy to see it. And then they took me to Ellis Island, there was a crowd of people there and they talked and talked, one talked like this, the other talked like that, they all spoke a different language, but to me, to me they spoke English.

GP: You didn't speak English back then?

Mrs. G: No. Only "yes" and "no."

GP: So what happened to you on Ellis Island?

Mrs. G: It was pretty strange for me, with all those people, always those big groups of people. I waited for my sisters to come and get me. In the meantime they asked me a lot of questions: Where do you come from? So I told them, "I come from here and there." And then all of a sudden someone said, "Who are these people?" And I answered, "That's my sister, and he's my other sister's husband." They wanted to know all sorts of things: Why did you come to America, how much money did we have, because at the time you had to have such and such an amount of lire to be able to get in. Why? I still don't know. They were probably afraid that I couldn't even buy myself a piece of bread. I don't remember exactly how much, but in any case, I know I had it. Oh yes, I remember something else, they put a tag on us, here, with my name on it, like for cattle *(laughter)*.

GP: Do you remember the medical examinations?

Mrs. G: Ah yes, They looked at your eyes. Yes, especially the eyes. Otherwise they didn't let you in.

GP: You spent the entire day on Ellis Island?

Mrs. G: Almost all day, yes. Then I remember, we took the boat with my sister, the small boat and the Third Avenue train. At the time it was elevated.(…) If there was anything that really amazed me, it was all the ads in the streets and everywhere—there were prices for all sorts of things everywhere. For me it was something new, because I had never seen that in Italy. And then we went to my sister's place. At the time she lived on 199th Street.(…) Less than a year later, I got married and I moved to the Bronx and from the Bronx we came down to the Village. And next September tenth, it'll be fifty-four years that I live in the same building.

GP: The same apartment?

Mrs. G: Oh no, not exactly the same apartment, because I used to be in number 18 and now I'm in number 16. My son was born there.

GP: What was your work?

Mrs. G: Here? Well, I sewed. And my first job was in the largest store here, it's famous, Franklin Simon. I only stayed three or four months, then it was the dead season, so I looked for another job.

GP: Were you paid by the piece?

Mrs. G: Oh no, not back then. Do you want to know how much I earned a week? You want me to tell you? Three dollars a week! Ha! What do you say about that! Sure, it was enough to buy a piece of bread. Anyway, nobody could say that I had money from the start!

GP: You earned some later?

Mrs. G: Well, I got married. In 1917: May 5, 1917. My husband was Italian too, but he was born in America.

GP: What did he do?

Mrs. G: His specialty was woodworking, inlays, you know, with all the little pieces of wood. But he couldn't find that type of work here, so he worked as a carpenter. That wasn't really his trade, so then he found himself a small shop and repaired old furniture. Very, very well. He had very good hands. Everyone liked him. He worked for very rich people.(…)

GP: Did you want to go back to Italy?

Mrs. G: I went back. In 1930.

REMEMBRANCES

GP: Did you plan on staying?
Mrs. G: No, no, no, no.
It was just a visit.

GP: To see your mother?
Mrs. G: Actually, it was to see my father. He was still alive when we decided to go. But while I was getting my papers together for the trip, my father died, so I didn't get to see him. My son was four-and-a-half when I took him there.

GP: You wanted to show him to his grandmother?
Mrs. G: Oh yes, she was very proud of him.

GP: How long did you stay?
Mrs. G: I came back after about three months.
  (…)

GP: How many children did you have?
Mrs. G: Only two; one I lost when he was six years old, the other is fifty-three now.

GP: What does he do?
Mrs. G: He's a history professor. He went to Fordham University and then to Columbia.

GP: Does he live in New York?
Mrs. G: No, he's in Washington.

GP: Do you have grandchildren?
Mrs. G: I only have six.

GP: Are they in Washington, too?
Do you visit them?
Mrs. G: Oh yes. As a matter of fact, he just called me, he wanted me to come; one of his daughters just finished high school; the last one, yes. All the others are in college.
GP: Have they been to Italy?
Mrs. G: No, only my son. I took him when he was four-and-a-half, but that's it.

GP: Does he speak Italian?
Mrs. G: Yes. I always spoke to him in Italian until he went to school. And then I learned English at the same time he did, by making him repeat his lessons.

GP: And your grandchildren, do they speak Italian?
Mrs. G: No, no, no, not even a word.

GP: Not a word?
Mrs. G: No.

GP: What do you think of that?
Mrs. G: The only thing they can say is "*Nonna*," it means "Grandma" in Italian. You know, when I send them something for their exams, I always sign "*Nonna*," never "Grandma." I like signing "*Nonna*."

GP: I thank you very much, "*Nonna*."
Mrs. G: You're welcome. I am very happy…. My son would like to know when the film will be shown because he's dying to see his mother on television….

~

MRS. CROCE

Arrived from Italy in 1912, at fifteen-and-a-half

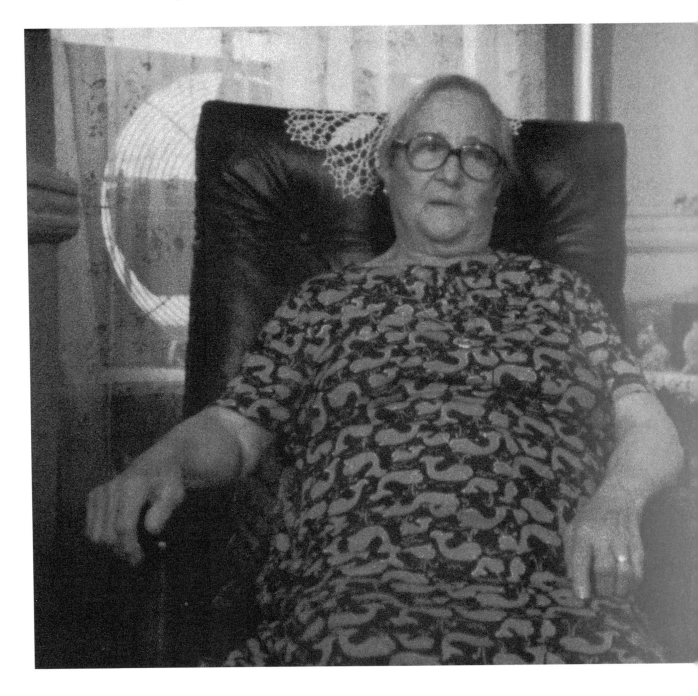

REMEMBRANCES

We met Mrs. Tessie Croce at a party at the senior citizen's center of St. Anthony's, in Greenwich Village, where she volunteers during the preparations for their annual festival. The interview took place late in the afternoon on Thursday, May 31, in her home.

GP: When did you come to America?
Mrs. Croce: In 1912.

GP: How old were you?
Mrs. C: Fifteen-and-a-half.

GP: Were you born in Italy?
Mrs. C: I was born in Italy, yes.

GP: What did your father do?
Mrs. C: My father was a carpenter.

GP: And why did you go to America?
Mrs. C: Well, it was bad over there. There was no way to earn money, so my uncle sent for me here, my mother's brother; he had come over many years before.

GP: Did you come with your whole family?
Mrs. C: No. Only three of us. My grandmother, my mother's mother, my aunt, and me.

GP: And your mother?
Mrs. C: My mother came later, a lot later, I think she came in 1922.

GP: Did you come from the north of Italy?
Mrs. C: We took the boat at Genoa.

GP: Do you remember the trip?
Mrs. C: Oh, of course. It was rough. The food was bad. You couldn't even eat at a table. We used to ate like beggars there, we ate sitting on the floor, with our plates next to us. It was terrible. White tin plates.

GP: You were in third class, in steerage?
Mrs. C: Yes, that's it. My grandmother was in second class, because she was old, but we were in third class. We couldn't afford to spend more.

REMEMBRANCES

GP: And then you got to Ellis Island?
Mrs. C: We spent the last night on the tug boat and the next day they took us over to Ellis Island.

GP: How was it?
Mrs. C: Awful. I wouldn't go back for anything in the world. It was terrible! So many people, so many people! Oh my God! It looked like cattle all over the place…

GP: What happened?
Mrs. C: We waited for the medical examination; they examined your eyes, they checked to make sure everything was O.K. If it wasn't they sent you back. If your eyes were red or something like that, they sent you back. But thank God I was healthy!

GP: Was your uncle waiting for you?
Mrs. C: He came to get us, yes, he took us to his place—he lived at 75 Vestry Street, it's very close, in the neighborhood; he always lived in this neighborhood. He's dead now. He went back to Italy and he died. My grandmother's dead too, and my aunt…

GP: Your uncle went back to live in Italy?
Mrs. C: Yes, he got married, he went back there and stayed…

GP: And you, did you ever plan to…?
Mrs. C: I made a home for myself here and then I had my two brothers come and then my mother. Now she's dead; her, too.

GP: What was your profession?
Mrs. C: When I got here, I found work in men's suits. Finishing suits at five dollars a week.

GP: Had you been working in Italy?
Mrs. C: I used to help my mother, and then I went to Turin.

GP: To go to school?
Mrs. C: No, not to school, to work…To work for the rich people, that was my job—shop for groceries, wash clothes, wash the floors. Here I did everything, men's suits, dresses, and then I worked in a pasta factory…lasagna.

GP: Like in Italy?
Mrs. C: Exactly. Except that they were made here, in America.

GP: Have you worked your whole life?
Mrs. C: All my life. Since I was ten-and-a-half years old. I worked until about seven years ago.

GP: You retired seven years ago?
Mrs. C: My last job was in flowers, artificial flowers…. I'll tell you again, I did all kinds of trades. You had to work if you wanted to eat. That's all.

GP: How old were you when you got married?
Mrs. C: I was twenty-two. I had a good husband. Now it's almost nineteen years that he's gone…

GP: What did he do for a living?
Mrs. C: He worked in a wine factory…. In our country, they make a lot of wine, you know.

GP: He was from Italy too?
Mrs. C: Yes, he arrived the same year I did, but I didn't know him.

GP: How did you meet him?
Mrs. C: He lived in a room in the same building as me, on the floor downstairs.
GP: Were there a lot of Italians in your building?
Mrs. C: It was at a friend of my uncle's, who came from the same village he did. My husband was a boarder of his. At that time, people rented out rooms to boarders because it helped pay the rent. That's how we met and we got married. There.

REMEMBRANCES

GP: Did you have children?

Mrs. C: I had two children, a boy and a girl. I had three children, actually, but one died. She was a month old and caught whooping cough. At that time they didn't have all they do now. Today doctors perform miracles. But back then, they didn't know much about it. So she died, that's all. And I have two grandchildren and two great-grandchildren.

GP: What do your children do?

Mrs. C: My son is a mechanic and my daughter is a dressmaker.

GP: Like you.

Mrs. C: Like me, yes, but she went to school. And my grandson is eighteen and my other one is an electrical engineer and he has two girls, two little girls. That's my family.

GP: Are you pleased with your family?

Mrs. C: Of course. I have good children and grandchildren.

GP: Do they live in New York?

Mrs. C: My daughter lives in Brooklyn and my son lives in New Jersey and my grandson lives on Long Island. They're all over the place.

GP: They're all scattered but not too far away...

Mrs. C: No, not too far away...we call each other, and we see each other sometimes.... (...)

GP: Did you go to get your mother at Ellis Island when she came in 1922?

Mrs. C: Yes, but she came over in second class, so she came out almost right away.... She came with my sister-in-law, my future sister-in-law. You see, my brother was already here, I brought him over just after the war and he had my mother come over with his future wife.

GP: They had met in Italy and he came over first?

Mrs. C: Yes, he came over first and then he had her come. They were married on the island. Back then, that's the way it was done; before getting into the country they had to get married. So she came with my mother and my other brother, the little one.

GP: Your whole family came?

Mrs. C: Everyone, except for one sister. She still lives in Italy. She's older than me; she's also a widow but she never wanted to come over. I kept saying, "Come, I can find work for you and you'll be able to retire," but she didn't want to. She may come for a visit. I got a letter from her this morning.

GP: Have you gone back to Italy?

Mrs. C: Yes, I've gone over two or three times.

GP: But you didn't want to go back to live there?

Mrs. C: No, it's another life over there. I'm so used to it here. In Italy, I only have a sister and some distant cousins. I'd rather be with all my family here.

GP: Have you ever thought that your life would be different if you had stayed in Italy?

Mrs. C: No.... I wouldn't have liked it.... I don't care for Italy any more. There are too many communists there, too many things that I don't like. Here, it's a free country. *God Bless America!* That's all.

∼

MRS. RABINOVICI

Our last interview took place in Paris, in September of 1979. 250,000 immigrants were rejected from Ellis Island. The ships that had brought them were required to take them back to their ports of origin. Some of them returned to the towns where they were born. Others did not dare return. One such case was Robert Bober's great-grandfather, who, thinking luck was on his side, had shaved his beard before arriving on Ellis Island. They found he had trachoma, however, and he was automatically rejected. He did not want to return to Przemysl (near Lemberg) beardless, so he stayed in Vienna until his beard grew back. Some years later, after the *Anschluss*, his granddaughter Frances Doniger, an Austrian refugee, left for America via London. We had never imagined that it would be possible to meet someone who had been sent back from Ellis Island. However, a series of coincidences and near-miraculous circumstances led us to Mrs. Rabinovici. She left Romania at fifteen with her older sister. They were unaccompanied, and were refused entry because they were too young and there was no one in the United States to take them in. Both were sent back to Hamburg. From there, they returned to their native town. A younger sister left for America after World War I and was allowed to enter. Years later, Mrs. Rabinovici went to live in France, in Paris, in the 18th *arrondissement* (district). She has lived alone since then but maintains many contacts in the United States, where she has often visited her sister and nephews.

During our interview, we were struck above all by the impression that she saw her experience as a failure, a lost chance that never should have been refused her. In America, she told us, you are invited to become American. "Here, after forty-seven years," she said, "I have not yet succeeded in becoming a citizen." Before we left, Mrs. Rabinovici showed us a house plant that she had brought from her last trip to New York and that had since sprouted one new leaf.

~

ACKNOWLEDGMENTS

We are grateful to the following organizations for their cooperation:
Archives Pathé, Bettman Archives, Greenwich House, American
Museum of Immigration, Museum of Migrating People (Bronx),
Museum of the City of New York, National Park Administration,
National Park Service Ellis Island Immigration Museum, especially
Barry Moreno, New York Public Library, Our Lady of Pompeii,
Photo Glenn Supply, Tamiment Library NYU, Library of Congress,
Weiner Library (London), YIVO
as well as
Sarah Adlerstein, Louie Balducci, John Blum, Baruch Chasimow,
Tessie Croce, Blanche Fried, Pierina Gasperetti, Maxine Groffsky,
Jane Kakis, Simone Kaplan, Peter Lerner, Morris Merow, Antonio
Mosca, Guiseppe Piegari, Anna Rabinovici, Suzy Rollins, Chaim
Lipa and George Rubman, Roselyn Schwartz, Rose Schwartz,
Semyon Shimin, Nathan Solomon, Aniello Tufano, Max Zeldner;
and Jean-Claude Brisson, Blanche Cuniot, François Ede, Dominique
Forgue, Claude Fréchède, Claude Guisard, Jacques Pamart, Claude
Pezet, Ellen Spiegel, Monique Villechenoux.

The publisher is grateful for permission to use the following
copyrighted images. Numbers indicate pages in this book on which
they appear. The rest were taken by the film crew.
68-69, 86: © Harlingue-Viollet. Courtesy of Roger-Viollet.
30-31, 74, 75, 87: Burt Phillips. © Museum of the City of New York.
75, 85, 88, 89: Courtesy of United States History, Local History and
Genealogy Division; The New York Public Library; Astor, Lennox
and Tilden Foundations.
76, 77, 78, 79, 80, 81, 82, 83, 84, 91, 92: Courtesy of the Lewis W.
Hine Collection; United States History, Local History and
Genealogy Division; New York Public Library; Astor, Lenox and
Tilden Foundations.
93: Courtesy of the William Williams Collection; United States
History, Local History and Genealogy Division; New York Public
Library; Astor, Lenox and Tilden Foundations.

The New Press extends its thanks to the French Ministry
of Culture and Communication for its translation support and to
Institut National de l'Audiovisuel.

BIBLIOGRAPHY

Hundreds of texts, including many works of fiction, describe, evoke, or analyze European immigration to the United States. Here, we are citing only those we consulted most.

Dasnoy, Philippe. *Vingt Millions d'Immigrants*. Elsevier Sequoia, 1977.

Ertel, Rachel. Élise Marienstras and Geneviève Fabre. *En Marge*. Maspéro, 1976.

Karp, Abraham J. *Golden Door to America: The Jewish Immigrant Experience*. Penguin Books, 1977.

Kessner Thomas. *The Golden Door: Italian and Jewish Immigrant Mobility in New York City* 1880-1915. Oxford University Press, 1977.

Metzker, Isaac Ed. *A Bintel Brief*. Ballantine, 1971.

Novotny, Anna. *Strangers at the Door*. Bantam, 1971.

Wakin, Edward. *The Immigrant Experience. Faith, Hope, and the Golden Door*. Our Sunday Visitor, 1977.

May 1979, setting up Lewis W. Hine's photographs
for use in the filming of Récits d'Ellis Island.